CW00571356

DYSART IN DAYS GONE BY
VOLUME TWO
Jim Swan and Carol McNeill

Pan Ha' 1891

THE DYSART TRUST

© The Dysart Trust 2013

Published by The Dysart Trust.

ISBN 978-0-9530213-3-8

The Dysart Trust gratefully acknowledges the support of Fife Historic Buildings Trust and Fife Council in making this publication possible.

All images are from the archives of the Dysart Trust and private collections.

The Dysart Trust is a recognised Scottish Charity No. SC 133137
www.dysart-trust.org.uk

Printed by Multiprint (Scotland) Limited
www.multiprint.tv

Contents

A Bit of Old Dysart

Dame Dysart's Lament

I met a woefu' fate yestreen,
Foregaithered in the Normand Ha',
A daidly stroke atween the een,
I'm left wi' scarce a breath tae draw.

Fur mony centuries I've thrived,
Until the hindmost year or twa;
Gainst mony a blast I've bravely strived,
But noo my prestige's stown awa'.

Nae mair Conventions wull I see,
Nor Burgh's rank will I possess;
Relegated I tae Cooncillors three,
Sans Provost, Baillies – cud it be less?

Had I foreseen in days bygane,
Kirkcaldy's Third Ward hud been mine;
The Pairish o' my name they've ta'en -
Amalgamation's been my bane.

Wa'es me! I'm but a washed oot rag,
My banner's trodden underfoot.
"Desertum." Has no a hame tae brag,
A ruthless law has pit tae rout.

"St. Serf"

This poem appeared in the Fife Free Press on 18th January 1930.
It was written after a meeting of Dysart Town Council made the decision to
amalgamate with the Burgh of Kirkcaldy, ending over four centuries of Dysart's
status as an independent Royal Burgh.

Dysart In Days Gone By

Introduction

This second volume of Dysart in Days Gone By includes the part of Dysart not featured in the first volume. This covers upper Dysart, which, in comparison with lower Dysart, is of relatively modern construction, most properties having been built in the late 19th / early 20th centuries. Most of the houses there were built in a time of relative prosperity among the business and trades community and reflect the newly found affluence which was to cease with the outbreak of the First World War in 1914.

The next phase of house building was in the 1930s with the construction of social housing in Cook Street, Stewart Street, Edington Place, the Walk and Bellfield Crescent. The majority of these houses were occupied by families from lower Dysart who were moved out of sub-standard housing which was subsequently demolished, changing the old familiar town forever. The 1960s and 1970s saw the second transformation of the town, with what was left of the old properties bulldozed and modern flats built to replace them. The recent demolition of some of these flats in High Street, Fitzroy Place and Fitzroy Street, and the construction of housing more in keeping with the character of the old town is the latest step in the transformation of Dysart. Hopefully, this will be a continuing process in the future when financial conditions improve.

The section on Clubs and Organisations covers most of the social organisations that once existed, which were so essential to the life of a thriving community. That so many of them have gone is an indication of how society has changed over the past half century but those that remain still play an important social and recreational part in the lives of the people of Dysart.

The miscellaneous section is just that, an eclectic mix of items from the archives of the Dysart Trust. Much of this material would not be accessible in any other form as they are among the bits and pieces accumulated over the past 49 years since the Trust was founded in 1964. 2014 will mark the Dysart Trust's first half century and our main aim, to collect, research, publish and generally make known the history of our town will hopefully continue.

Jim Swan and Carol McNeill, 2013

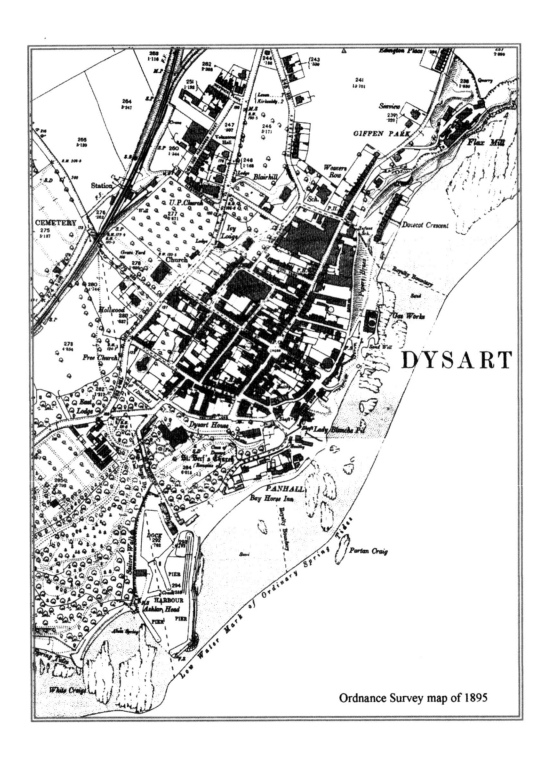

DYSART

Ordnance Survey map of 1895

2

Top of the Town

BARONY
CHURCH
DYSART.

Up to 1802, when Dysart Parish Church was built, there were few buildings above what is now Normand Road. The land stretching west to Sinclairtown, north to Gallatown and as far as Thornton, was given over to farming and the agriculture necessary to feed the people and animals of the Burgh. A large portion of the ground was called 'the Town's Garden' and was divided into plots rented to the inhabitants to grow fruit and vegetables. The Barony, as the church was later named, replaced old St. Serf's at the shore which had become inadequate to serve the congregation. Worship ceased at the Barony in 1977, five years after its merger with St. Serf's, West Port. It was used for some years by the YMCA as a sports venue and it is now intended to convert it into flats. Right, a commemorative bookmark issued in 1941 to mark the death of Rev. Hugh Menzies who had served as minister for 36 years.

Townhead 1900. The Royal Hotel had large stables behind it from where horses and all kinds of carriages could be hired. It had previously been called the Railway Hotel, dating back to 1847, when the railway first came through to Dysart.

Top of the Town

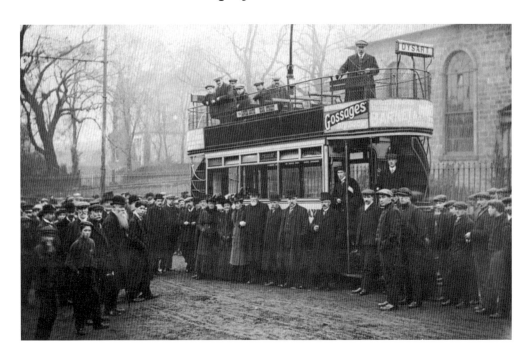

19th of January 1911. Dysart's first tram at the terminus at Townhead in front of the Barony Church. A large crowd gathered to greet the arrival of the tram, including Provost Anderson, prominent business men and other luminaries of the town. They all got on board for a return trip along Dysart Road to the Cottage Hospital opposite the bottom of St Clair Street.

Townhead 1912. A tram stands at the terminus. The road, which was formerly a dirt surface, has been laid with granite setts imported into Dysart Harbour from Aberdeen. The newly built Bank of Scotland is on the right. The Dysart branch had previously been at the Cross where the Post Office is now.

Top of the Town

Townhead 1912. The ivy clad tower with the flagpole was at the top of East Port and once guarded the main entrance into Dysart when it was a walled town. It dated back to the early 16th century and was partly dismantled in 1926, the remains being incorporated into the house and shop built there.

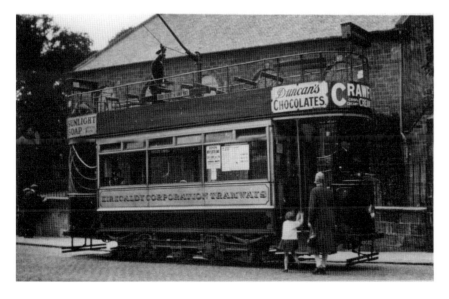

At the terminus towards the end of the tram service. Competition from bus companies eventually saw the end of the trams on May 15th 1931.

Townhead 1888. The saddler's shop of James Macleod, on the right in front of the door. He took over the business from Peter Hitt after working for him for six years. He was elected to the Town Council in 1902, made a Baillie in 1909 and became Provost in 1919, a position he held till 1930 when Dysart ceased to be a Royal Burgh and amalgamated with Kirkcaldy.

In 1898 James Macleod moved to larger premises on Normand Road.

Top of the Town

A trade advertising card c.1910.

c.1928. A float entered in the Kirkcaldy Pageant, Provost Macleod at the reins. This event was held annually to raise funds for the Cottage Hospital.

Provost Macleod wearing the Dysart
chain of office, 1920.

Top of the Town

The Royal Hotel c.1890. This painting, looking along Townhead from the top of East Port, was painted by an itinerant artist called 'Pedlar Palmer' who often exchanged his work for the price of a few drinks in the local hostelries. He travelled the east coast extensively but seems to have favoured Dysart as there are many of his works here.

A receipt from the Royal Hotel stables for the hire of horses and carriages for a wedding party.

Top of the Town

Townhead 1948. Not many people had cars then. Blyth's shop is on the right.

After Macleod the saddler moved to new premises, the Blyth family moved into the building and opened a small shop selling groceries and sweets.

Above, the Dysart Gala Queen for 1955, Sheila Davidson, passes Blyth's shop on her way to lay flowers at the War Memorial.

Left, the Blyth family 1900. Maggie Blyth, who was the last to run the shop, is second from the left.

Top of the Town

Terrace Street, Dysart.

Looking up Terrace Street c.1912. The buildings of Dysart Station can be seen at the top of the street. Most of the houses in upper Dysart were built between 1880 and 1914, including those at Normand Road, Terrace Street, Watt Street, Alexander Street, Berwick Place, Fraser Place, and Hill Street. They were occupied in the main, by middle class and business people. Terrace Street was named after Andrew Terrace, linen manufacturer and Provost of Dysart from 1886 to 1896.

Watt Street c.1912. Watt Street ran from the top of Terrace Street to the top of Station Road. It was named after David Watt, master baker, who was Provost of Dysart from 1870 to 1886. All of the houses in Watt Street, the right hand side of Terrace Street, Station Road and Alexander Street, were eventually demolished due to damage caused by mining subsidence.

Top of the Town

Normand Road c.1914. Typical of the houses built for business men was 'Craignaw', on the left, commissioned by David Watt in 1908. He was the son of David Watt who was Provost and carried on the family bakery business in High Street after the death of his father.

'Craignaw' 1928.

Top of the Town

Normand Road c.1920. Normand Road. U.F. Church was built in 1867 at a cost of £2,600. It replaced the old church in Relief Street which was not large enough for the congregation of the time. It closed in October 2009, the congregation having fallen to just 28 members. The building was sold for redevelopment.

One of the oldest buildings in Normand Road is Eden Valley Lodge. This was built c.1840 to serve as the gatehouse for Ivy Lodge, a large Georgian mansion, once home to the Normand family who had three linen mills in Dysart. It has carved stone birds on top of the gables.

Top of the Town

Normand Road c.1912. Normand Brae is on the left, the bottom of Station Road is on the right. The railings on the garden walls were taken away for scrap to make weapons during the First World War. The photographers of these postcards always seemed to be able to round up a group of children to give more animation to their photos.

This 1926 view shows one of the few cars in Dysart at this time.

Top of the Town

Dysart Primary School. Opened in 1916 and originally called Blairhill School. It was one of three schools in Dysart at that time, the others being the Infant School at School Brae and the South School on High Street.

OOR SKULE
When ye gang in the mornin',
The Maister says a prayer,
Syne ye get yer singin lesson,
An roar till yer thrapples sair,
Weel! Syne ye gets yer jography,
Wi' the pointer in yer haunds,
On the map tae show oor Dysert,
Exactly whaur it staunds.

Fancy Dress Parade at Blairhill, 15th of June 1918. The proceeds of a collection taken during this event were used to send comforts to the British troops in France, the First World War still having three months to run.

Top of the Town

Normand Road at the top of Hill Street c.1908. There were two shops on the right hand side at this time, on the corner of Fraser Place, and further down, on the corner of Berwick Place in the red sandstone buildings. Both shops are still there.

Top of Hill Street c.1908.

Top of the Town

The newly opened Dysart Co-operative Society building c.1934. With a long established presence in the High Street, the Normand Road Co-op filled the need for serving the expansion of upper Dysart in the 1930s where new housing schemes were built at Cook Street, Stewart Street and Bellfield Crescent. There were butcher, baker and grocery departments.

The staff of the Normand Road Co-op c.1948.

Top of the Town

The Courier
January 30th 1912

An alarming incident occurred on the mineral railway leading to the Frances Pit, Dysart. A train consisting of ten coal-laden wagons had been left standing on the line when for some unexplained cause it ran off down the incline towards the pit. The gates at the level crossing on Wemyss Road were knocked down by the runaway train which continued its career to the pithead of the Frances, about half a mile further on where it struck the corner of the joiner's shop, which was demolished by the impact.

The 'White Gates'. At the end of Normand Road and the beginning of Wemyss Road, the rail line which these level crossing gates controlled ran from the sidings at Dysart station to the pit head of the Frances Colliery. When coal was being moved from the colliery, motorists sometimes had to wait for long periods when the gates were closed.

c.1967. A diesel locomotive hauls coal wagons to the sidings at the station. The gates were removed in 1984.

Frances Colliery 1974. A colliery work engine starts to haul filled coal wagons up to the White Gates and the Dysart Station sidings from where it would be transported to the customer. This all came to an end in 1981 when the Frances and Seafield Colliery in Kirkcaldy were linked underground and all coal from the two pits were transported from Seafield. Frances closed in 1985 and Seafield in 1988.

1966. A steam engine leaves Dysart Station loaded with a long string of coal wagons.

Top of the Town

Scottish Oil Depot, Wemyss Road. The last buildings past the White Gates leaving Dysart, the depot was built in 1925. It distributed B.P. products all over Fife and beyond, including petrol, kerosene, heating oil and lubricants. It closed in 1987.

Armistice Day Parade c.1955. It was long the practice for the ex-servicemen of Dysart to march around the town on Armistice Sunday morning before arriving at the War Memorial at Townhead to lay wreaths and remember the fallen of two World Wars. The photo was taken at the top of Cook Street with the Oil Depot in the background on the right.

Top of the Town

Dysart Station 1908. Built in 1847 when the railway first came to Fife. This photo is looking north, next stop Thornton.

Railway staff at Dysart Station c.1902. The policeman on the right was one of Dysart's own police force, stationed at Victoria Street and consisting of an inspector, a sergeant and two constables.

Top of the Town

Above, c.1904, a crowd of day trippers, probably from one of Dysart's three linen mills, wait on the north side of the station for a train to take them on their annual works outing. These trips were paid for by their employers and were in the days before paid holidays. Newburgh and Ladybank were two popular destinations.

Right, a novelty postcard posted in 1916 to Edinburgh by 'Jessie' in Dysart. The message says "If you come here on Thursday, we will be on the lookout for you. There is a train which leaves Waverly at 10.15 and arrives here at 11.48am, so we will meet that one. You will have to be on your best behaviour, because we have turned over a new leaf!" Intriguing.

I shall look out for you at DYSART

Top of the Town

Dysart Station 1959. In only ten years time the station would be shut down as part of the Beeching cuts, the last train stopping there at seven minutes past midnight on Monday October 6th 1969. The signal box operated for a further 11 years.

1960. A steam train leaves the station belching steam and smoke. This photo was taken from the footbridge between Bellfield Crescent and Berwick Place which was built in 1949. Up to then, passengers had to use a subway running under the line to get from one platform to the other. The footpath in front of Bellfield Crescent is on the right.

Top of the Town

These views of Edington Place were taken in 1968 shortly before demolition. The rows were built in 1866 to house workers in the linen mills in Dysart. The new houses built on the site in 1974 were mostly sheltered housing for elderly people. To the east of Edington Place there was a row of houses called 'The Braes' which belonged to the Coal Board. These were demolished about the same time and the Frances Mining Memorial now stands on that site.

Clubs and Organisations

Dysart Golf Club, opening day, 1898. Situated on the west side of Dysart Cemetery and extending from Loughborough Road to Gallatown and Windmill Road. The first ball was struck by J. Oswald, Dunnikier House. A nine hole course, it actually lay outwith Dysart in Kirkcaldy Burgh Boundaries. It was in existence till 1950 when the course was used for house building.

Above, a later photo of the clubhouse after it was extended in 1900.

Left, the clubhouse in 1952 as a two storey building. Looking down towards Loughborough Road, the railway line and Lady Nairn Avenue.

Clubs and Organisations

Dysart Bowling Cub c.1930. The club was founded in 1914 at Townhead on ground which was formerly a quarry. Lady Nairn from Dysart House played the first bowl and the first President was Provost James Oswald Anderson who was also elected in the two following years. The clubhouse was extended in 1993.

Opening of the season c.1967. The spire of Dysart Kirk is in the background.

Clubs and Organisations

Windmill Road Old Men's Club c.1948. The clubhouse was behind the manse of what was then St. Serf's Church at Townhead. Entry was off Windmill Road behind where Lady Nairn Avenue is now. Sir Michael Nairn, who gifted the ground where the hut was, is 6th from the left and Baillie John Cook is 2nd from right. When the houses at Lady Nairn Avenue were built, the members moved to the White Gates Old Men's Club hut in Normand Road.

Group photo of the members of the club. They held weekly whist and domino tournaments and organised other social events. Members' wives also attended.

Clubs and Organisations

Dysart Rifle Club c.1964, at Station Road. Back, l to r. D. Wilson, J. Williamson, J. Harley, J. Copeland. Front l to r. J. Campbell, W. Scott, N. Lumsden. The rifle club started off in an old flax spinning mill at Edington Place. A tragic accident occurred there in December 1951 during a raging gale, when the gable of the building collapsed on the rifle range. Two of the members were killed and two were injured, all young men. Another man who went to help took ill and later died. The club later moved to Station Road in one of the old railway buildings.

Dysart Cycling Club, 1934. Setting off for a run at the foot of School Brae. The Man I' The Rock is on the right, part of Meikle's carpet factory is on the left.

Clubs and Organisations

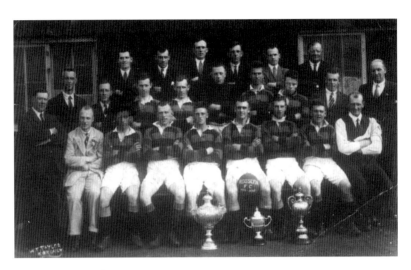

Rosslyn Junior Football Club. This football team had their pitch at Station Park at Windmill Road, where Windmill Place is now, and played in the Fife Junior League. Pictured above is the team of 1929-1930 when they won the Fife Cup, The Fife League Cup and the Cowdenbeath Cup. Back row. J. Hardie, G. Barclay, T. Mill, G. Robertson, W. Mckay, R. Wilson, middle row, W. Gillespie, D. Don, A. Mitchell, J. Pollock, D. Robertson, J. Rae, P. Ronan, J. McGuin, D. Thomson, Club President. Front row. M. Grubb, Vice President, J. Philp, Match Secretary, D. Adams, F. Robertson, J. Penman, J. Sharp, J. Murphy, P. Hood, A. Low, trainer.

Players and officials of Rosslyn Juniors c.1934. The houses in the background are at newly built Bellfield Crescent. Baillie Charles Bellfield, Club President is on the right of the front row.

Clubs and Organisations

Boreland Amateur Football Team, at the end of the1950 season when they had won every trophy in the Kirkcaldy & District Amateur League. Back row. G. McLean, C. Wallace, A. Sanaghan, T. Spence, S. Burns, C. Cummings, S. Gibb, S. Lynch, P. Heggie, A. McLean. Front row. D. Barclay, Secretary, R. Drysdale, President, W. Stewart, J. Cooper, G. McPherson, O. Mills, J. McNab, W. Barclay, trainer, J. Wallace. The photo was taken at Station Park.

Dysart School Football Team 1951-1952.

Clubs and Organisations

QUOITING - A NEW STAR IN THE FIRMAMENT.

Instances have not infrequently been recorded in history of men who got up in the morning to find themselves famous. This is the fate that has overtaken 'Dod' Harris, the youngest member of the Dysart Quoiting Club. In the club's monthly handicap, by which means the members keep themselves up to concert pitch, and are prepared to accept any challenge that is reasonable and has a ten pound note behind it. Harris was drawn against Charlie Marr, a player who was an easy first at West Wemyss Athletic Sports only a month ago. 'Dod', being a dark horse, was known to be well in with a start of 18 out of the 21, of which the game consisted. Marr being also favourably dealt with, getting 15. 'Dod's' first shot was a beauty, what quoiters call a 'Wubber', and he won the end. His next two quoits went nowhere in particular, but as they were somewhere in the vicinity, while Charlie's wasn't, he got the two shots and all was over bar the shouting, which was tremendously loud and long. 'Dod's' win at first caused blank consternation, then another shout arose sufficient to bring down the walls of Jericho if that ancient fortification had not been already laid low. Marr took this defeat badly, and immediately challenged the winner for a substantial sum. The enthusiasm was now unbounded. About a score of men were fighting for the honour of cleaning his quoits, one man in a fit of abstraction tearing his jacket into dusters in order to do so. The second game, like the first, ended in a win for 'Dod' amid tremendous excitement and scenes of jubilation not witnessed in Dysart since the end of the Boer War. 'Dod' Harris is surely a quoiting star of the future and Dysart will surely clean up every competition it enters with him in its team.

The Fife Free Press
August 3rd 1907.

Dysart Quoiting Club 1907. Quoits was a very popular game in the late 19th and early 20th century. It was played on a pitch with a clay pit at one end with a steel pin stuck in it. The object was to ring the pin with the quoit. Dysart won the Kirkcaldy & District League Championship Cup with the above team. Their clubhouse and quoiting pitch was at Edington Place in a field above the old quarry but many matches were played at the harbour.

A group of quoiters at the quoit ground at Dysart Harbour c.1928. This was on the west side of the 'Oil Shed'. They are holding 'placers', smaller versions of the full size quoits, which were thrown at a piece of paper on the clay bed. l to r. J. Allan, T. Carrington, K. Henderson, J. Bruce, R. Grubb, A. Wherle, C. Archibald, R. Christie. H. Christie, R. Allan, R.Young, D. Grubb, W. Lawson, A. Littlejohn, R. Bruce, D. McNeill.

Clubs and Organisations

Dysart Scouts and Cubs of the 35th Fife (Dysart) Troop c.1925. The group was photographed behind St. Serf's Church at West Port. The 16th century 'doocot' is still there at the end of the War Memorial gardens.

Cubs at the Scout Hut in Fitzroy Place / Rectory Lane 1949. The hut was demolished in 1965 to allow houses to be built on the site. The Troop used the Normand Hall and Dysart Town Hall before moving to a new Scout Hall at Quarry Brae.

Clubs and Organisations

Scouts and Cubs photographed at the playground in West Quality Street 1937.

Clubs and Organisations

35th Dysart Scout Group pictured in their hall at Quarry Brae on the Troop's 50th anniversary in 1975.

Clubs and Organisations

Dysart Guides c.1925.

Clubs and Organisations

1st Dysart Girl Guides 1945. Pictured at the playground with St. Serf's Church in the background.

Clubs and Organisations

1st Dysart Brownies at the top of Falkland Hill, Pack Summer Camp at Falkland School July 1955. Those who attended were: Brown Owl, Miss M. Meikle, Grey Owl, Miss I. Prentice, Camp Cook, Miss C. Traill, Brownies: I. Clark, C. Whyte, M. Reid, S. Lumsden, C. Reid, J. Dickson, A. McMillan, N. Cairns, F. Addison, S. Thomson.

Brownies from Dysart, Viewforth Church and Pathhead packs gather to celebrate the 75th anniversary of the founding of the Brownies, 1989.

Clubs and Organisations

Dysart Town Band outside Perth City Halls 1910. The band, which was formed in 1880, was very successful in competitions and played at many local Gala Days, especially at the band stand at the Dubbie Braes.

They were supported by Dysart Town Council and several wealthy benefactors. After Dysart amalgamated with Kirkcaldy in 1930, the band was then supported by the miners in the Frances and Randolph Collieries who gave one penny from their wages per week and the band was renamed The Dysart Colliery Band.

Dysart Colliery Band 1942. Photographed in the playground at the 'Wee School' at School Brae. The band still continues to be successful today as the Dysart Colliery Silver Band.

Clubs and Organisations

The Dysart Trust was formed in December 1964 after a meeting in the Relief Street Hall. The meeting was called after a very successful exhibition in April 1964, called Dysart of Yesterday, was held in the Normand Hall. This had been organised by the three churches in Dysart, St. Serf's, The Barony and Normand Road, to raise funds for Freedom from Hunger, to send aid to Africa. So successfully attended was the exhibition and so great was the interest shown in Dysart's past that it was decided to form a body to collect, preserve and display material relating to the long history of Dysart. A committee was duly elected and work got under way immediately. The Trust's first objective was to get permission from Kirkcaldy Town Council to open St. Serf's Tower to the public. This was granted and for nearly fifty years this, along with the many exhibitions held in various halls in Dysart, were the Trust's main activities. The first year the Tower was open at weekends from April to September, over a thousand people visited. Other activities included entering a float in the Kirkcaldy Hospital Pageant, organising an annual bonfire and firework display at the harbour and facilitating an annual open air service in the body of the old kirk by the shore. Many publications have been produced with the historical material researched and photographs collected over the years. The Trust continues to work to collect and make known material relating to Dysart's long history. The above photo was taken in the cemetery of St. Serf's in January 1965 and shows the original committee. Back row l to r. John McLean, William Smith, John Ross, Albert Kidd, Charles Alexander, Jim Swan, Robert Patterson, Frank Trimmer, Peter Jamieson, Hamish King.
Front row l to r. Mrs. John Grubb, Mrs. Violet Grubb, Robert Cunningham, Mrs. Jean Cunningham, Mrs. Alice Jamieson.

Clubs and Organisations

The Trust's float for Kirkcaldy Pageant 1965. Dysart was once known as 'Little Holland' because of its trading links with the Low Countries. The junior members of the Trust won many prizes with the float.

Part of the current Trust exhibition in Dysart Town Hall. The Trust has been based in the Town Hall since the early 1980s and the exhibition is open on Sunday afternoons from July to September, or at other times by appointment.

Clubs and Organisations

Dysart Boating Club was founded in 1933. It ran races for yawls, skiffs and square stern boats and the annual regatta was keenly contested with boats from Dysart, West Wemyss, East Wemyss, Buckhaven and Kirkcaldy competing. Sports for the children were also organised at the Piper's Braes.

The harbour 1938. Three of the boats which competed in the yawl racing, 'Rover', 'Amateur' and 'Isabella' in the trinket. The owner of the 'Isabella', Wull Carr, caused a sensation when he built a cabin on his boat so he could take his wife sailing in comfort. He received so much criticism from other yawl owners that the cabin was removed for the next season's racing!

Clubs and Organisations

1942. The yawl 'Jim' sets off for a sail. The 'Jim' was built in Leith in 1908 for the Proctor family of Dysart. It is now in the small boats collection in the Fisheries Museum in Anstruther. Note the high narrow footpath at the wall at the Aisler.

Regatta day 1948. Boats getting ready to race consult with the Commodore's boat concerning the course to be sailed. The boat at the right was the 'Roulleta', one of the boats stored at the harbour during the Second World War and later scrapped.

Clubs and Organisations

Dysart Sailing Club was formed in March 1967. When it took over the harbour it was badly silted up by waste from the nearby Frances Colliery. This picture of the east pier shows the structure as it was then.

An exceptionally fierce easterly storm in April 1969 washed away the outer end of the east pier closing off the harbour entrance. To the newly established Sailing Club this presented huge problems as their total assets amounted to only £300.

Clubs and Organisations

This view shows the damage caused by the storm a few days after it subsided. The masonry remaining on the left had to be removed by using explosives in order to clear away the rubble from the entrance.

1970. Looking from the Tarry Sands towards the harbour entrance after the remaining rubble had been cleared. The harbour was left vulnerable to storms and swells from the south and west. A navy ship sails by the harbour.

Clubs and Organisations

Efforts to raise funding to rebuild the east pier started almost immediately after the storm but it was not till August 1973 that work started. The project, to rebuild with steel piles, cost £30,000, and was funded by The Scottish Sports Council, Kirkcaldy Town Council and Dysart Sailing Club. At the time, it was hoped to rebuild with stone, but the extra £5,000 cost of this could not be raised.

Driving the last pile, October 1973. The pier was topped with a concrete deck and officially opened in November 1973. It has since had another row of steel piles driven around the outside because the original steel was badly corroded and the deck has been renewed twice because of storm damage.

Clubs and Organisations

In June 1972, the club was host to the Scottish & North of England Osprey Championships. It attracted an entry of 34 boats, most of them local but some from as far distant as Cornwall. The Osprey was the fast class boat adopted by the club and at one time there was a fleet of 15 boats based at Dysart.

September 1974 saw Dysart host the Scottish Mirror Dinghy Championships. 60 boats competed over the weekend. This shows part of the fleet on the beach behind the east pier ready to launch for a race.

Clubs and Organisations

This 1977 view shows the harbour still badly silted up. Efforts to clear the harbour continue annually, especially at the entrance after winter storms.

2011. The inner dock has been cleared of thousands of tons of mud and the harbour is now full of boats. The club continues to grow. The Oil Shed on the right, Dysart Sailing Club's clubhouse since 1996, was regrettably gutted by fire in January 2012. Efforts are ongoing to raise funds to refurbish the building.

Clubs and Organisations

Lodge St. Clair of Dysart No. 520 was formed in May 1872. Meetings were first held in The Subscription School and then in the old Town Hall. In 1890, the 5th Earl of Rosslyn who had been appointed RWM on two occasions, gave as a gift, the former Free Church building for use as a permanent home for Lodge 520. Extensive alterations were required to the building and it was not till 1893 that meetings were held there.

Brother David Hume the first
RWM of Lodge St. Clair.

The plaque above the door
commemorating the gift of the hall.

Miscellaneous

The following is from the English Illustrated Magazine for 1891.

AN OLD FIFE BURGH TOWN.

By DAVID S. MELDRUM.

With Illustrations by H. R. BLOOMER.

HE " saut burgh " of Dysart is and was a typical Fife coast town. From its Hie Gait, in the centre of which was the Square with its Cross and tollbooth and the spacious piazzas, where, in olden days, the merchants displayed their wares, many narrow and tortuous streets, well described, in their physical features, by their common name of " wynds," slope down to the quaintest of old-world Fife harbours. Despite its notorious want of safety (which, indeed, did not matter much in days when mariners sailed the seas for half the year only, and lay up, with their boats, for the winter on whatever shore the end of summer found them), this harbour, from an early date, was crowded with craft. These, for the most part, plied a trade with the Low Countries. The principal exports were salt and coals. Dysart supplied the neighbouring towns also with both commodities. In 1659, for example, we find an order to Lord Sinclair's " factor " at Desart to furnish Edinburgh Castle with 1,000 loads of coal, the bailies of Desart to transport them to Leith. In an Act of the Scottish Parliament, nearly a century previously to that, reference is made to Lord Sinclair's " coal-pot " in Dysart. As for salt, " ca'in' saut to Dysart " has long been as contemptuous a proverb as " carrying coals to Newcastle." In return for the exports were imported all the necessaries and luxuries of life which Bruges could supply. Russian furs, fine Flemish cloths, and wines from Spain and Italy came for the courtiers at Dunfermline and at Falkland ; wax for the Church, and, as time rolled on, Bibles for the Reformers ; pitch, tar, and wood ; and even old iron for the Pathhead nailers. So important was the Fife continental trade that when Bruges, after being for three hundred years the market of Northern Europe, declined in favour of Antwerp, the Scots became possessed of privileges very similar to those of the Hanseatics. In the town of Campvere, close to Antwerp, for example, there is said to have been a Scotch Gate, through which Scottish sailors passed " Scot free," while those of other nationalities paid toll. Indeed, so jealous was the Government of these rights that it appointed an official, who was known as the " Conservator of Scots' privileges at Campvere " ; and it is of interest to note that such an official existed as late as 1758 in the person of no less illustrious a man than John Home, the author of *Douglas*. So much for the foreign trade. At home the mealmakers, fleshers, shoemakers, tailors, and brewers carried on thriving businesses under the protective privileges of the crafts. Altogether, so industrious and wealthy did Dysart become that it was known as Little Holland, a title which might, with equal fitness, have been applied to the whole seaboard from Inverkeithing to Crail. It would be wrong, however, to think of the Fife towns as quite sordid in their interests : content to grub away at trade and barter and to leave it to others to fight the battles of liberty and of religious freedom. It was not so. Fife led the van of

civilization in Scotland, and was in a condition of comparative peace and plenty when the remainder of the country was in the throes of civil strife. It is a tribute to Fife that when a proof was wanted of the success of the efforts of James V. to restore the Borders to law and order, it was put forward that he received as good an account of his sheep which fed in Ettrick Forest *as if they had grazed in the bounds of Fife.* But her merchant sons could fight as valiantly as the Lubeckers. Flodden and Drumclog meant the loss of fathers and sons to her towns. As a matter of fact every foot of Fifeshire is historic ground.

THE OLD TOWER OF S. SERF'S.

Tradition associates this corner of the coast in a marked way with the vagaries of the devil, and legend has it that St. Serf became the patron saint of Dysart by ejecting the devil from a cave in the vicinity of the town. He seems to have done so by means of persuasive argument. In his *Cronykil* old Prior Andrew Wyntoun gives us examples of the patron saint's powers in this direction, and they make it no surprise to us that the devil fled to escape them. This cave is now inclosed within the grounds of the Earl of Rosslyn's Dysart house. Walking on the shore one sunny afternoon, the present writer "got on the crack" with an old native. Pointing towards where the cave was, the native expressed a desire to see it. "It's no' worth your while gaun to 't; some story o' an auld sanct's been the makin' o't," was the contemptuous opinion. But although even the vulgar now affect to speak slightingly of the "auld sanct," his name was once powerful in the town. The parish church was dedicated to him; and at the town council elections "kirk masters" and "compost masters" were chosen to receive "St. Serf's money."

The hold which the Church had upon the town is very evident. Some fifty yards to the eastwards of the harbour there is a cluster of stone and lime which is a record of centuries. The old Norman tower has survived the church to which it was attached, even as the grave-stones have the memories of those whose bones lie beneath them. A blacksmith plies his trade within the walls of what was once the chapel of St. Denis; and all that remains to mark the home of the Black Friars is a gateway upon whose lintel there may yet be distinguished, through many coats of lamp-black, the superscription in relief, "My hope is in the Lord." This gateway leads into an unused courtyard, o'ergrown with grass, in the midst of which is a pit-shaft, kept open to ventilate the present workings on the hill. The quaint building built into the wall of

Miscellaneous

this gateway is now a tavern whose small rooms could doubtless tell many a tale of smuggling and the sea. To complete the record there are numerous cellars built into the old ruins, which have been salt-gurnels and straw-lofts in their day, although their doors now never open upon their rusty hinges, while, straggling to the water's edge, may yet be seen the foundations of salt-pans—the very ones—who knows?—which the Earl gave in dowery long ago, and were known as "Lady Jane's pincushion."

The Church and trade, and more interesting still, the municipal polity, and the relationships of man with man, whose character is seen in the very frequent enactments of law-burrows, or bonds not to molest one's neighbour; all these have light thrown upon them in the interesting burgh records. These books, dating from 1533, by which time Dysart had become a royal burgh, are among the most ancient of their kind in Scotland They are rendered especially interesting by the fact that Dysart, with its rector and vicar and some half-dozen of chaplains, was an ecclesiastical centre, and, therefore, much resorted to in days when commercial transactions

DYSART.

took place in the church. Previously to receiving a Royal charter, it had been a barony burgh holding of the Sinclairs, of whom we shall hear more. The disposition of these burghs may be taken as a sign of the relative power of the Crown and of the nobility. The Crown won an ally in a corporation to which it granted a charter; and it frequently found itself strong enough to step in and raise to the rank of a royal burgh a burgh of barony which had become great and wealthy. This is what seems to have taken place in the case of Dysart. When it was raised to the higher rank it was the seventh or eighth town in Scotland. It possessed so much wealth and influence, as compared with some neighbouring towns, which have far outrun it in the race, that down to a recent date there was a common saying: "The gentlemen of Dysart and the men of Kirkcaldy."

Let us turn to these records, then, for a knowledge of the old Fife burgh. Its affairs were conducted by two bailies and a varying body of councillors, who, sitting as the head court, made statutes and ordained. There is no means of knowing if the "sett" of the burgh was fixed by charter; it certainly came to vary considerably, for in 1535 there were fifteen councillors, while thirty years later there were no fewer than forty. Nor did they hold office voluntarily. Statutes of the head court decreed that "whilk of the persons (chosen as councillors) bides away from the council being lawfully warnit by ye officer, and they have not received leave, shall be fined ilk time five shillings, except they are reponed." At the same time we find the tyranny of the guilds in full force, " nae unfree man nor unfree woman" being allowed " to occupy freeman's freedom in baking or brewing or any other thing of freemen's occupation under pain of eight shillings as oft as they bake. . . ." In the records of the burgh of Kirkcaldy the undemocratic aim of separating the occupants of civic chairs from sordid employments, noticed by Dr. Hill Burton, the historian, finds illustration in the fining of Provost Robert White for brewing ale in his own house.

A note in the records fixes for us the summer of 1576 as the date of the building of the present townhouse or tollbooth. Where the old one was situated we do not know ; but it seems probable that, for long, it was in bad repair. For forty years, at any rate, before the new one was built, the minutes of council are dated from the steeple ; from "under John Kilgor's stair ; at ye foreland of Arch. Halkitt ; under the stair of umqwhile John Abernethy" ; and from "the Market Cross."

The duties of a bailie within his bailzerie consisted chiefly in the prevention and punishment of crime. The old powers of "pit and gallows," delegated to feudal lords, were likewise in the hands of the constituted authority of a royal burgh : we find "pain of death" frequently threatened, at least, if not inflicted. Ordinary offences were covered by a system of fines. We may, at least, suppose that there was a system whereby the punishment was made to fit the crime, and that it was a relic of the Anglo-Saxon scale of money value in which each member of the community was assigned a place according to his social position. One unfortunate man, John Kilgor by name, was sentenced to be "wardit and joggit and furyr, for his contention and na comperance, to be dowkit in ye sea." Alexander Stirk, for assaulting the officer and breaking out of prison, was sent to the "joggies," or pillory, and made to stand there "but meit or drink till sax hours at even, and theirafter gif he commits the like fault to be banest the town for ever." Bell Wood for entertaining beggars was sent to the "cuckstule." The minutes of the court are too vague to enable us to exactly understand the constitution of a jury. It is just possible that the bailie, besides being judge, acted as public prosecutor. The chancellor of the assize certainly passed sentence after the verdict was found. We may be allowed to quote from another entry which throws a light upon the desire for fairness in the administration of the law. "The whilk day John Orkney, prolocutor for Margaret Brown his wife, protested that David Blair, bailie, should be nae judge to him nor yet his wife, because that the said bailie and they were not at one." In these minutes and records of head courts and assize we get a glimpse of the practical working of that spirit of humanity which was a distinguishing characteristic of old Scots law.

The actual administration of the law, however, must have been faulty. The modern police is a physical force which the solitary doomster, or officer of court of those days, could not possibly be. The bailies themselves assisted their officers, and passed laws binding "ye haill nybors to be in readiness and defend yaer common weills." Repeated instructions by the magistrates to every booth-holder to have in readiness within the booth "ane jack, ane halbert and steel bonnet for eschewing of sic inconveniences as may happen," may have been made necessary by "inconveniences" from within the burgh as well as by those from without. The town's officer deserves a notice if for no other reason than that he is the precursor of that most original of Scottish worthies, the minister's man or beadle. Although it is not borne out in the Dysart records, there are grounds for the belief that in many cases the office passed from father to son. In a Scottish county-town at the present day there is an old man who is pointed out as the hereditary hangman. We have seen that the doomster, although only a servant, was sworn in along with the bailies ; and in several cases of breach of the peace we find the offenders praying for forgiveness on their knees before the magistrates, and on their feet before the officer. As bellman, he warned the councillors to their meetings. As church officer he had to "toyme (empty) the kirk by day ilk Saturday, and to keep the kirk, by prayer and preaching, with a long wand in his hand." It would seem that one of these officials distressed the neighbours (the word appears so kindly) by charging exorbitant prices for burials ; whereupon the following scale of charges was fixed : forty shillings Scots for every corpse buried in the kirk ; for every corpse buried in the kirkyard, having a coffin, twenty shillings ; for young children, thirteen shillings and four pennies ; and for a corpse without a coffin, ten shillings. The same statute "appointed the said bellman to bury the puir corps, either strangers or inhabitants and parochoners, gratis." As time wore on, the duties of the Dysart gravedigger became onerous, and he was compelled to furnish, at his own expense, a man to break the

Miscellaneous

ground. This assistant, however, who was "an able man," undertook other duties whose nature may be inferred from his *sobriquet* of "buff-the-beggars."

The strict measures adopted by the guilds to prevent outsiders encroaching upon their trading rights made the burgess ticket of considerable value; and it is evident that a dividing line was firmly drawn between servants and unfreemen and those who occupied "freeman's freedom within the burgh." Accustomed as we are to free trade, we can have little idea of the tyranny of the guilds. Naturally, as a burgh increased in importance, and the burghers became wealthier, they became also more imbued with the spirit of money-making, and allowed their greed to protect their own industries to an extent that led to the downfall of the whole system. At the same time, while those guild laws limited the production they guarded the quality, and protected the people from extortion. Take, as an illustration of this, the decree: "that no white bread be baken by ony baxter hereof but leven bread, guid and sufficient stuff, under ye pain of eight shillings; and yat no baxter hereof, nor nane in his name, tak for baking of ane

boll of victuall but . . . shillings, all other charges discharged, and ye nybors to be thankfully served." Of a like nature is the order that no flesher should pass to land-ward to any place where the sickness was among cattle, or to suspected places to buy cattle to slay and sell.

The precautions against the spread of fire, which the old burgh laws reveal, are a proof that most of the houses were constructed of wood. In the middle of the six-teenth century, however, at which time the new tollbooth was erected, a considerable amount of building was being carried on. If we can judge by the inventories and roup lists which have been preserved, the furnishing of the houses at this time was of the meanest description.

In Dysart, previously to the Reformation, there was probably one ecclesiastic for every hundred souls. Shortly after that event a fellow-labourer was brought in to assist the clergyman; and mention is made of a "reader," whose stipend was fixed at twenty pounds. The position of the schoolmaster was more precarious. It was in the year 1600 that the first qualified teacher was provided for the town. Twenty-six years later Mr. John Gow, who then held the office, drew up a petition setting forth that it was the usual custom for the parents by turns to supply the school doctor with meat, and that, as he had been prohibited from enforcing this, he was entitled to extra salary by way of compensation. His representation was favourably entertained and he got four shillings (Scots) quarterly from the parents in addition to his stipend. In order

Miscellaneous

to further better his position it was decreed: "that na woman, mistress of a school, should receive male children who were able to attend the hie school." Some thirty years afterwards this worthy man's successor was fined and deposed for striking one of the neighbours to the effusion of blood.

These glimpses into this old Fife burgh show us only a busy, shrewd, worldly community. In reality that is the dull ground on which the patterns of romance must be worked. From such a home as this went forth the lads who, with levelled spears, stood shoulder to shoulder round their bonnie Prince at Flodden. Not only the maids in the sheep-folds of the Borders, but those mariners' and craftsmen's daughters also, mourned "with dule and woe the lads who were a' wede awa."

The mention of the men who marched to Flodden with Lord Henry Sinclair is the first authentic one in which Dysart is seen in touch with the history of Scotland. We have earlier traditions of battles with the Danes and of repulses of English marauders from the shore; but from this point the historical associations of the town are numerous, and for the most part are, like this one of Flodden, bound up with "the lordly line of high St. Clair." About a mile westwards from the town stands the old home of this family, the now stately ruin of Ravenscraig; so harmoniously set into its background of trees and rocks that from the seawards it may easily pass unnoticed. Lifted high on its rocky pile it commands the Firth, which now mirrors it in its quiet waters, now beats against its old walls as on that night when the lovely Rosabelle ventured from its shelter for Roslin's halls.

We can best deal with the historical associations of Dysart by observing where its fortunes joined issue with those of the Lords of Ravenscraig. It affected the burgh but little that Oliver Sinclair, the third son of Oliver of Roslin, and an old servant of James V., was raised (much to the chagrin of the nobles) to the command of the Scots army when it crossed the Borders. It was defeated in the rout of Solway Moss, and the unhappy monarch died with the moan upon his lips: "Fy! Is Oliver fled? Oh, fled Oliver." But among those curious inventories of goods and gear to which we have already referred, is one: "Ane Kyst, ane cruik, ane speit, ane tangs, ane spynning wheel quhilk brunt by the Frenchmen." This occurs in 1563, and is a curious confirmation of the presence of the French troops which Mary of Guise brought over to oppose the forces of the Lords of the Congregation. The harrying of the coasts of Fife by those soldiers hastened on events as did also, no doubt, the burning of Walter Mylne by the priests. Lyndsay of Pitscottie says that Mylne was arrested in Dysart by the vicar, Sir George Strachan,[1] "in ane poor wyfe's house, teaching hir the commandments of God, and learning her how she should instruct hir bairns and hir household and bring them up in the fear of God." Taken before the judges, "Thou preachest quietly and privately in houses and openly in fields," the public prosecutor said to him. "Yae, man, and on the sea also, sailing in ships," Mylne answered. There was "grit" in the words. The annals of these religious struggles can furnish a literature which will testify for ever to the greatness of the Scottish language. Walter Mylne was burned; and at the Reformation which soon followed George Strachan ceased to be vicar. He turned his attention to dealings in peat and to the manufacture of salt. History cannot always be written in heroics.

The three meetings of the Synod of Fife, held in Dysart in 1607, illustrate the kind of fight which Presbyterianism had to make against the episcopal designs of James VI. That sovereign desired the appointment of constant moderators, in which the Presbyters saw the rise of Bishops. The first of these meetings was held on the shore between the town and Ravenscraig, the church being shut against it. Two months later the Synod was convened in the church, and again in August. On the last occasion the retiring moderator was Mr. William Cranstoun, whose duty it was, in ordinary course, to preach the sermon. Archbishop Gladstanes, of St. Andrews, and the Commissioners, however, interdicted him from doing so. The scene which followed must have been a curious one, although doubtless it was serious enough to all engaged in it. Mr. Cranstoun had mounted the pulpit, when a messenger delivered the interdict to him. To it, and to a similar second message, he paid no heed. Then, even as might have happened at the present day, a little municipal authority was tried, and a bailie of the town went to the moderator and told him that the Commissioners ordered him down. "And I command you," replied Cranstoun, "to sit down in your own seat and hear what God will say to you." The Netherlands Consul next interfered,

---

[1] The title "Sir" was a mark of courtesy to the vicar.

but he succeeded no better. " The Lord and His Kirk have appointed me ; therefore beware ye trouble that work," was the answer he got. The moderator preached his sermon, in which he did not hesitate to handle the Archbishop severely ; whereupon the prelate is said to have stormed so outrageously that even the Commissioners "were fain to tell him that he was unworthy to be in the number of ministers."

It is startling to be reminded by a visit, paid by the Marquis of Huntly, or one of his train, to old Sinclair of Ravenscraig, one early morning in February, fourteen years before this, that at the time that questions of religion and of Church polity were thus agitating the country a brutal murder, which raised the indignation of all classes, could be condoned by the King. The visitor had come from Inverkeithing that morning, leaving behind him the smouldering ruins of Donnibristle, and the " bonny Earl of Murray," lying dead along with the gallant and faithful Dunbar. Birrel in his *Diary* relates the murder in graphic words : " The 7 of February the Earle of

RAVENSCRAIG.

Huntly came to the hous of Dunnibirsell in Fyffe, quher the Earl of Murray with a few number wes for the tyme, being his awen house. The chieffe man yat wes with him was Dunbar, Shriffe of Murray. The Earll of Huntly sett ye said hous on fyre. The Earll of Murray being within, vist not quhither to come out and be slaine or be burned quicke ; yet after advysment this Dunbar says to my Lord of Murray, ' I vill goe out at ye gaitt before your lordshipe, and I am sure the people will chairge on me thinking me to be zour lordship, sua, it being mirke under nycht, ze shall come out after me and look if yat ye can fend for zourself.' " Dunbar did as he proposed and was slain, while in the *mêlée* the Earl of Murray fled to the rocks on the shore ; " but, unfortunattly, the said Lord's cnapscull tippet, quherone ves a silk stringe, had taken fire, vich betrayed him to hes enemies in ye darknesse of ye night, himselve not knowing the same ; they came down one him on a suddaine and ther most cruelly, without mercy, murthered him." It is said that it was not the private feud between Murray and Huntly alone that instigated this murder, but that the young Queen Anne had praised the beauty of the Earl too freely ; at any rate the King, in spite of the entreaties of the victim's mother, and the outspoken indignation of the capital, retarded the prosecution of Huntly and finally hushed the matter up. The avowed motive for this murder ; the reason which the popular voice gave for it—that " he was the Queene's luve ; " the self-sacrifice of Dunbar, who is the only hero of the story ; the picturesque

Miscellaneous

discovery of Murray among the rocks by the burning fringe of his tippet; the murderer pursuing his way along the Fife coast, and being received by Sinclair of Ravenscraig with the words: "Since ye have come to my door I cannot shut it upon you, but on such business you would be welcome to have gone past it;" the dying words of the vain if bonny Earl: "Ye have spoiled a better face than your own;" the grief of his mother and her almost melodramatic way of showing it and of demanding revenge: these all give to the story of this tragedy a wealth of colour which it would be found difficult to match.

The first Protestant minster of Dysart, and in a sense, therefore, George Strachan's successor, was William Murray. He was related to the Tullibardine family, through whose influence his son received a post in the household of Charles I. Gaining the favour of his royal master, his rise was rapid, and in 1651 Charles II created him Earl of Dysart.

Meanwhile Cromwell had invaded Scotland. Fife suffered greatly. Bad seasons had sent up the price of provisions. The plague was spreading, and we find the magistracy of Dysart giving orders "to close up the town's ports, with sufficient yetts (gates), bands, and locks; and all the open places of the burgh presently to be biggit up with stane and lime." Four regiments were raised from the county in twelve months, and no fewer than twelve of horse and five of foot quartered on it. The castle of the Sinclairs is said to have been occupied by Cromwell's troops, and afterwards left in ruins by them, and local records afford numerous proofs of oppression. No doubt Fife and the Fifeshire towns would welcome Charles II in his progress through here in 1651.

Sixty-five years later the Earl of Mar, landing at Elie, negotiated with the Fifeshire lairds in favour of another Stuart, and finally raising the standard of revolt, marched on Perth and captured it. Amongst those who helped him was the young Master of Sinclair, who brought with him a body of cavalry. To Mar's standard came most of the Highland chiefs. One, the Duke of Sutherland, remained conspicuously loyal. He ordered his ships, with stores, to sail round to Dunrobin; but the winds being contrary, the captain thought to visit his home before proceeding, and anchored off Burntisland. News of this reached Perth. The Master of Sinclair rode to the shore, boarded the vessel, captured the stores, and carried them off to the rebels. The rising of 1715 was a failure, and the Master had to flee; but he lived to a good old age, and wrote memoirs of the insurrection which were published by his descendant, the late Lord Rosslyn, whose daughter, not many years ago, married an heir of that Duke of Sutherland whose ship the Master captured.

The rebellion of 1745 marks the close of a great period of Scottish history. From this point men and women take the place of parchment and records as authorities; and the only qualification that is asked of them is that they shall have talked with men who were out in the '45, and so are able to join hands with the past in the memory of what their fathers have told them.

After the union of the kingdoms, the Fife coast towns lost much of their prestige; and their history in the past one hundred and fifty years has been one either of decay or of a rise, in new prosperity, from the ashes of the old. But we have failed in our purpose if we have not suggested to the reader a brighter, if still a homely enough, patch than that which must generally be painted in the picture of Scotland.

Miscellaneous

From The Illustrated London News of June 28th 1862. An artist's impression of fishing boats off Dysart. This headed an article about the plentiful supply of herring in the Forth.

Thoughts
on
Boyhood Days in Dysart

By John Terrace
Of Toronto, Canada.

John Terrace emigrated to Canada with his family in 1905. His father was the manager of Terrace's linen factory, the Viewforth Works, situated between the High Street and the Piper's Braes. The factory was owned by his grandfather, John, who was Dysart Burgh Treasurer and his brother Andrew who was Provost of Dysart. It closed in 1904.

The reminiscences came about through correspondence in 1957 with P.K. Livingstone, a Kirkcaldy author of books such as "Flax and Linen in Fife", 1950, and "A History of Kirkcaldy - 1843 - 1949", 1955.

Thoughts on Boyhood Days in Dysart

In common with many old Dysart lads and lassies, I am greatly indebted to Alex Logan for his interesting and vivid articles in the Fife Free Press. They have stirred up in me a lot of old memories - things I have not thought about for many years.

Although only as a pupil at John Boyd's school, I too played football on Fowler's field and at the Dubbie Braes. We had recurring ambitions to become a real team, and made several attempts to collect enough money for football strips but we never got beyond the stage of discarding our jackets and piling them in heaps to mark the goals. This led to many disputes over the unorthodox decision of 'a post'.

Our football was always more or less lopsided, and we had considerably difficulty on inflating it by lung power, in which we all shared. If we could only have acquired one of the new beauties in Macleod the saddler's shop window. One Saturday afternoon we played against a team from Guthrie's School in Nether Street, Pathhead, and our defeat rankled for many weeks.

My first school was the South School, and the fees were discontinued while I was there. In the room downstairs, facing the Vennel, we were taught the alphabet and I recall when I read "the cat is on the mat" and similar phrases for the first time. Other memories are the abacus with its red and blue balls strung on its wires, and chanting the multiplication tables. Our teachers were Miss Terrace and Miss Anderson.

Later on we were moved upstairs into the large room divided by a glass partition. There were pictures, some of whales, on the walls, and in a glass case, a bees' honeycomb, a small sheaf of flax and other things. There was also a map of Scotland in high relief.

Eventually we graduated to John Boyd's school at School Brae and it must have been about this time when Normands built the Calendar factory, as I have a recollection of a chimney stack being demolished and of building operations. The new plant was lit by electricity, its first appearance in Dysart, probably about 1890. John Boyd was headmaster and his staff included James Anderson, James Boyd, William McGregor, Miss Wright and Miss Nicholson - all strict disciplinarians who used the tawse generously but never unfairly.

In the playground we kicked a ball of newspaper bound with string; played 'wecht' and other games. In due season we made reins from coloured worsted; and bools, girds, kites popguns and hawspittles came and went in that mysterious sequence of which we were unaware.

We had drill once or twice a week, first under Sergeant Wherle and later under Sergeant Capel, both ex-military men. 'White Wings, they never grow weary', 'Scots Wha Hae' and 'Bonny Dundee' were the accompaniments we sang to the various exercises.

Two brothers named Robinson repaired shoes near the South School. One of them had a curious trait. If you looked back at him after you had met and passed him, you found that he was looking back too. Then he put his thumb to his nose and spread his fingers out. Needless to say, we always took full advantage of his peculiarity.

In 1890 there was a public gathering in the grounds of Dysart House to celebrate the 21st birthday of the present Earl (the 5th Earl of Rosslyn). There were fireworks, and I was small enough to be somewhat terrified by the large crowd. The old Earl (the 4th Earl of Rosslyn), died later that year and there was an impressive ceremony in the Parish Kirk, which was draped in purple and black. My grandfather used to describe the church as being built in 1800, costing £1800 and seating 1800. I remember the building of the organ, which replaced the harmonium played by Miss Simpson. James Gray was the first organist.

The Duke of Cambridge, Commander-in-Chief of the British Army, attended a service in the Parish Church in the early 1890s. The Church Soirees were a great delight. Our tickets of admission entitled us to a 'poke' containing cookies, orange and apple, nuts and raisins and conversation lozenges. We tolerated the musical part of the programme, being mainly interested in the magic lantern show which was ably conducted by James Mitchell, School-Master of the Boreland School. The animated colour comic slides were, to us, the principal item, especially one of a sleeping man into whose open mouth a procession of mice disappeared.

The Band of Hope held weekly meetings. On one occasion we were addressed by one of the ministers who told us that one of us would make his mark in the world. After we came out, Andra Baxter claimed that the minister had referred to him and was ready to fight anyone who disputed it.

It seems to me that our lives were fully occupied when we were schoolboys, especially during the long days of summer. We had but few opportunities for travel and our world was limited to Dysart and its immediate vicinity. The foreshore was our great playground, and we knew every yard of it from Ravenscraig to the Blair Burn. We used to make unauthorised entries into the grounds of Dysart House and explore the old castle, under fear of being discovered by the gamekeeper.

My grandfather worked hard on the idea of having a sort of esplanade at the Back of the Aisler and even utilized the old dock gates in the scheme. There was a natural spring on the foreshore which still tasted of salt when uncovered by the tide, but at low water its true flavour– alum– was apparent. As I recall, there was about 18 feet between the high and low Spring tides. The trinket was the name of the channel from the dock to the harbour mouth. Captain Harrow was Harbour Master and we liked hearing him roaring out a command. Often ships had to lie inside the east pier because the dock was full of schooners. Sometimes these ships would be careened on the Tarry Sands and the crews, in long boots, set to work cleaning the hulls. There was considerable competition at one time between pilots in bringing in ships. This led to exciting races between light six-oared gigs, owned by Smith, Alex Cairns and Bob Cairns. The 'Lee', a three-masted ship came regularly for coal, and was a favourite because we were sometimes allowed on board, and occasionally got a ship's biscuit.

At one time a shipload of flax for the Old Mill was discharged and the Customs officer ran a thin blade (from his swordstick) through each bale as it was swung over, and would smell the blade - as we told one another whisperingly - to detect smuggled tobacco.

We were always greatly interested when the loaded ships went out. There was the full-bosomed tide; the opening of the dock gates; the straining of the crew on the ropes, and the slow steady progress of the ship; the piling up of a big hawser in a rowboat, then the capstan clicking as the ship was pulled to the entrance; another hawser in the boat, this time to be attached to the flat wooden buoy on the outside of the harbour; and finally the ship swinging around as sails were hoisted to catch the breeze and she was off.

Most of these ships were built either at Stavanger, Norway, or Marstal, Denmark. I recall looking with disfavour on the first small steamer to take out a cargo of coal. In my early days the dock was deepened, and we watched the blasting operations from the far end of the Sailors' Walk. A coffer dam was built so that the sill could be lowered and prepared for the new dock gates which had been built at the shipyard. Lord Rosslyn had a yacht named the 'Violet', but it spent most of its time on the cradle in the shipyard. I dimly remember the sound of caulking hammers and the launching of a new ship.

Certainly I helped on the capstan more than once to bring a ship up the slipway for repairs. A seven–day wonder was the yacht of the Duke of Sutherland, brother-in-law of the Earl of Rosslyn, which lay off the harbour for a while, with much traffic between it and the port.

Dysart boasted a good swimming club in these days when the only styles were the breast and side strokes. The annual swimming and diving competitions were very well attended and I have some recollection of sailing regattas held off the harbour.

Captain Harrow, the Harbour Master, lit a lamp of red glass at the sea end of the east pier every night. On one corner of his house there was a lamp of green glass, and pilots could bring in ships through the night, using both lamps as guides.

The old sawmill at the harbour was interesting. There were great logs lying on the brae east of the harbour waiting to be cut up by the screaming circular saws. I remember the old saw pits there being filled in as they were no longer required. Nets were dried at the Pan Ha' end of the brae and at least once the place was occupied by Bostock's Circus. The billboards then featured the untameable lion, 'Wallace'. We were thrilled when the lion tamer, with pistol on his hip, called for 'red hot iron bars' to keep the lion off while he entered the cage.

We dug bait and fished from the east pier, but our catches consisted of 'minnies' with only an occasional 'podlie'. The stretch from the 'Bay Horse Inn' to Dovecot Crescent, being faced by houses, was not much favoured by us as a playing ground. An exception, however, was the stretch of rocks at the Gas Works where we played 'cubbies', jumping from one rock to another when the tide was in. We always went home with squelching boots, and occasionally with soaked clothes.

My first voyage was made on a paddle steamer which carried Smith's mill workers on a trip to Alloa. We embarked from the east pier and I can still remember the strange feeling I had when the ropes were cast off and the pier began to move away from the steamer. We sailed under the Rail Bridge, then under construction, and the Italian workmen, perched like flies, threw down their caps (or were they rivet bags?) as we passed underneath.

Dovecot was a row of neat homes and the tenants took great pride in growing flowers and vegetables in their well kept gardens. From the 'Roondel' to Smith's Mill, brambles grew in profusion, but they were always picked in a green state. However, we used to hunt through the bushes in the hope of finding ripe fruit. My grandfather put up benches along there and at the Dubbie Braes.

The Dubbie Harbour, a large pool left when the tide went back, was our favourite place for a dook, and it was there that I learned to swim. There used to be two large ponds on the Dubbie Braes where we caught frogs. On the flat ground below the ponds there were some ruined buildings, once communal washing houses fed by natural springs. Nearby was the shooting range of the Dysart Volunteers. The target was off the Dubbie Harbour and the markers crouched under the shelter of a powder magazine. It was exciting to hear the whistle and thud of the bullets. I have also watched the marksmen from behind both of the 200 and 500-yard marks, the latter being a flat rock on the foreshore. The bull was made larger for longer distances. Sergeant Rankine and Corporal Graham were both good shots.

The annual review of the Volunteers was an exciting event, principally on account of firing the obsolete cannons. The charge, then the ball were rammed into the muzzle; the cannon was sighted, with much manoeuvring; then the sharp command to fire was given and there was a loud report, followed by the slow trajectory of the projectile towards the target. We played at Volunteers for weeks afterwards.

The Braes too were the scene of the Diamond Jubilee celebrations in 1897, and I recall the long wire rope hung with flags and the gigantic bonfire.

From the Dubbie harbour to the Red Rocks was where we played most, for there was where Jimmy Boyd, one of our teachers, often went with us for a whole day at a time. He owned a vest knife which had a curved blade, and was very sharp—price sixpence. With it he fashioned small boats from driftwood which we sailed across the harbour. He used to cut Y's from the whin bushes for gutties (catapults), and we put them under heavy stones to make them straight. We became fairly proficient at hitting targets of tin cans with stones from our gutties, stones which we selected with care from the beach. We spent hours up and down the cascade of hot water from the Dubbie pit, clearing out the ashes to make the streams run faster. The stream of cold water, larger in volume, we dammed and guided so that one day it would be running east, the next day west. Through the bushes along to the Red Rocks we made trails and played Red Indians. At low tide we explored the rocks for partans. We collected buckies and cooked them in a pan, borrowed from home, which we kept in a secret place. The same fire roasted tatties in the sand below. If it rained, we stood it as long as we could, then dried our jackets in the boiler room of the pit before going home.

We hunted for fossils and unconsciously acquired a little knowledge of geology. In the spring we gathered daffodils in the Blair Woods. One year, 1895, I think, a heavy storm breached the pier at West Wemyss harbour and strewed some half a dozen vessels along the foreshore.

During the winter our outside activities were curtailed by the short days and cold weather. When there was a frost (a rare occasion), some of the boys made toboggans and slid from the top of East Port down to the Cross. We also slid down School Brae in trucks - a line of boys sitting on their hunkers, each grasping the boy in front round the waist, and being guided down by "steersmen". In the field which later became the Dysart Golf Club were two old reservoirs, and I recall sliding on the ice there.

We played around the railway station frequently, as it was a very busy place in the old days with much shunting going on, which greatly interested us. An unusual event then was a train of coal wagons coming from the Dubbie pit. A kindly signalman took us into his cabin and explained the mysteries of his work. Boys came up for bundles of newspapers, and we pored over Comic Cuts and Alley Sloper in the bothy, where we also played Catch the Ten and other card games. There was only a shed on the north platform. Mr. Deas was the Stationmaster and filled the part well. William Young did all the railway carting. We had many a ride on his lorries and knew his horses by name.

There was a sawmill where the Bedding Factory now stands. It was run by a man called Chalmers, I think. There were bogies on rails from the mill to the railway sidings on which we used to ride.

The Royal Hotel was also a very busy place. The stables were full of horses and occasionally we were permitted to yoke up a horse to a brake, dogcart or carriage.

We used to be sent out on errands to the various shops. Besides these we went to the Tiend Barns for vegetables, but more often to Dewars on Normand Road—a cottage occupied by two old ladies. Their kitchen was immaculate, and a cool spot on a warm day, as it had a stone floor. Never were there such green peas, rasps and strawberries as their garden provided. There were other shops too, in which we had a more personal interest, such as George Watson's in Cross Street; Anderson's in Weaver's Row, where our occasional halfpennies were spent on snawbaws; Mairn Mitchies in Coal Yard, where she sold peaky balls, either white or crunchy, or the more popular brown and hard, as they lasted longer. Andra Ronaldson from the Gallatown peddled fruit from his cart. He had a stentorian voice which softened persuasively when he came to the door. A huge wagon from Star of Markinch came round occasionally, loaded with peat. The driver had a long brass horn which made a peculiar mooing sound.

Pete Hutchinson delivered milk from Fowler's dairy. From our windows we could see the cows being driven home to be milked. Cattle were herded down the East Port to be slaughtered, amid much shouting and barking of dogs. I could never get over a reluctance to look through a chink in the gate of the killing house in Victoria Street, but most boys did.

The Flower Show, in the nurseries at what is now Ravenscraig Park, was an important event. Men wearing badges on their coats took in tickets at the Lodge gates; there was the walk through the grounds to Three Trees Park; the close warm smell in the big tent, where the flowers, fruit and vegetables were displayed; there was a brass band. I also recall a display of tent pegging and cutting off the Turk's Head by members of the Fife Light Horse.

Living next to the manse (in East Quality Street), I knew it as well as my own home, as I played a great deal with the Gibson boys (sons of the Rev. Gibson, minister of the Parish Church). I also recall with gratitude that kind and gracious lady, their mother, who took such pride in her home and gardens, and worked indefatigably in all affairs connected with the Church, possibly the Girls' Friendly Society most of all.

I remember the row of old houses opposite being pulled down and replaced. We watched the stones being cut and faced with the various kinds of chisels and were quite sure we would all like to be stone masons.

We all knew Walter Smart, for in the autumn, he carried in the capacious pockets of his top coat, a supply of delicious pears. When he met us, and his mood was favourable, a pear was always produced. They were grown in his garden, and I recall the cool water from his well.

The Ostlere family lived at Ivy Lodge and the men were driven to and from Kirkcaldy by pedigree hackneys, whose names began with Moon—Moonlight, Moonbeam, etc. Dr. Goodenough occupied Blairhill and was driven around by his coachman, Aitken. Before my time Blairhill was occupied by the Normands, but I recall Patrick Hill Normand quietly distributing half crowns at certain houses along West Quality Street. Giffen Park was the home of the Livingstones. Mr Livingstone was later Provost of Dysart.

So in the 1890s, Dysart was a prosperous bustling community. In 1899, when I began to learn something of financial matters, the total distribution of money on pay days was very substantial. The retail merchants benefitted accordingly, and the general prosperity resulted in a number of new homes being built on Normand Road and elsewhere. Among those who moved into these were the Forresters (Chemist), Smiths (Grocer), King (Painter), Smarts (Butcher), Watts (Baker), and the Andersons (Mr. Anderson was later Provost of Dysart). The Harrows, Ramsays and Owlers remained where they were. I have a dim recollection of the building of Hollwood (James Herd), the Archibald house, Wilkie's house on Cross Street, Smith's house and his Flax Mill. Near the U.P. Church lived the Humes, close by the Boyds whose continued occupancy of Ardgarth must rank amongst the longest of any family in Dysart. Philip Clark, Thomas Harrow jnr. and his brother James, and the Duffs, had their homes in Berwick Place. On Hill Street lived Miss Munro, the Mitchells, Martins, Dryburghs and Boyds. On Quality Street the Laings, Forresters, Milnes, Gibsons, Terraces, Pyes and McNabs, the Alisons, Pattersons, Longs, Allans, MacNeils. Other familiar family names of that time were Ednie, Brodie, and Rankine on Cross Street, Hay and Bell, on Relief Street; the Misses Watt at the foot of Victoria Street; Glass, Wotherspoon, Drysdale, Foggo, John Watt, Robb, Buist, Blackater, Wilson and Westwater on High Street, and the names of Beall, Adamson, Langlands, Suttie, Duncan, Davidson, Johnstone, Mavor, Wallace, Christie, Galloway, Forker, Henderson, Macintosh, Syme, Maxwell, May, Page and Stewart will conjure up memories to those who lived in Dysart in these days.

John Terrace,
Toronto, Canada.

Miscellaneous

The Dysart Burgh Arms

Dysart's Burgh Arms. The oldest depiction of the civic arms is on the front of the stair leading up to the Tolbooth and Town Hall. It is now much worn by time and erosion but depicts a stylised thorn tree and the date 1617. The thorn tree, as local legend has it, grew on the moor to the north, between Dysart and Thornton. This was the spot where the local militia assembled with their arms in times of trouble. The village of Thornton is said to have taken its name from this tree. A variation of the Arms can be seen on the building east of the Tolbooth which was built as a Mechanics Institute in 1874.

The Dysart Seal

In 1895, Dysart Town Council adopted the above as the official seal to be used on Council documents. It again shows the thorn tree surrounded by the Latin motto meaning "sign of Dysart". Examples of it exist pressed into wax on important documents and embossed into the paper on others.

Miscellaneous

Dysart - The Origin of the Name

If your surname happens to be Dysart, it is unlikely that your forebears had any connection with this town. The family name would originally be D'Isart or D'Isert and your ancestors probably came over with William the Conqueror.

This town derives its name from the Latin noun 'desertum', or its plural form, 'deserta', a place of solitude.

Today's spelling appeared as far back as 1446, but the form which was common for a long time afterwards, and is embodied in the Burgh seal, 'Sigil de Dysert', was only indirectly derived from the Latin by the way of the Old French word 'desert'. This is first recorded, strangely enough, also in the days of the Conqueror, when there was a monastic retreat known as Le Desert de St. Bruno at La Grande Chartreuse near Grenoble in France.

There is a Dysart near Montrose; the name is common in Ireland, spelt Desert or Disert; and the parish of Glenorchy was Dysart or Glachandysert. On the island of Iona there is a Cladh-an-Disert (Gaelic, cladh, a graveyard) and also a Port-an-Disert.

The Rev. William Muir writing in his 'Antiquities of Dysart' in 1855, says, "Since we can find nothing in the name of Dysart expressive of its original appearance, or indicative of its antiquity, let us try other sources of information - from those I am disposed to think that the town was founded prior to the 9th century.

If it were so, the inhabitants must have had an uneasy seat, for it is certain that during the 8th and 9th centuries, the coast of Fife was frequently harassed by invasions of the Danes; and they are said to have often landed in the neighbourhood of Dysart.

I have often thought what could have attracted these invaders so often to the same spot - and it may have been in the caves that abound on our shore, these hardy invaders found a ready if temporary dwelling place, and also a natural stronghold to which they could remove their spoils, and keep them till the time of their departure.

There is no doubt that our shore has often been the scene of many a rough encounter with the Danes, but unfortunately for the inhabitants of Dysart, a more formidable enemy took possession of one their caves - this was the Devil!

Miscellaneous

There can be no doubt that they made efforts to eject so dreadful a tenant, and one who doubtless would make himself very troublesome, - but the inhabitants of Dysart were too timid to take effectual measures to eject him, or too weak to succeed. What then were they to do? Fortunately they thought of applying to St. Serf for aid, and sending a deputation to Portmoak imploring the aid of that Saint, he is said to have come to Dysart, and ejected the Devil from the cave!"

Thereafter, St. Serf is said to have spent time in spiritual contemplation in the cave. Such religious retreats were known in early ecclesiastical language as 'deserta,' and both in Scotland and Ireland the memory of their primitive occupants is kept up by the term 'Disert' or 'Dysart', which has been affixed to them.

The following poem recounts the battle in the cave by the shore between St. Serf and the Devil.

A legend from auld Dysart toon,
From years long gone was handed doon,
O' how it once was ruled by evil,
Hard in the grip o' Nick, the Devil;
And of the way which he was slain,
Then by Holy Saint in his death crypt lain.

Dysart, on the Forth's east shore,
Its fisher folk, simple and pure,
Who brought their harvest from the deep,
Their families to clothe and keep,
Did labour hard with line and creel,
With ne'er a thought o' black, dark, De'il!

The day was fine the Forth was calm,
The bairns in its waters swam,
When all went dark, and mighty storm,
Began upon the scene to form,
And chilling roar, like death's last knell,
"Kneel down before the King of Hell!"

I've brought thee misery and destruction,
Though luckless folk, my chosen faction,
Your lives shall lie in dismal shreds,
My eternal curse upon your heads,
Tis here I've chosen to reside,
Your hope and freedom, cast aside!

Beneath the evil Satan's yoke,
The downcast, harried, common folk,
Began to cast their eyes to heaven,
Of all true hope, they had been riven,
Yet one believed with true belief,
And gave his plan for their relief.

I've heard it said this man remarked,
That a Holy Saint has disembarked,
From oe'r the sea, from foreign land,
To preach his faith on Scotland's strand,
So to Loch Leven I'll now race,
To fetch the Saint, to this cursed place.

Miscellaneous

'Twas five long days, since he had gone,
As Satan's rule still lingered on,
Plagued by terror, want, starvation,
Death, disease, and cruel privation,
And from no hand had help been offered,
As 'neath the Black Lord's curse they suffered.

But then within their midst there came,
The Holy Man, whose saintly name,
Their brother true had brought to light,
Then put forth to the Saint their plight,
Behold good people, do not sigh,
For the power of the Lord is nigh.

Show me now where Satan bold,
Lurks within his dark stronghold,
Hie me there, do not delay,
His powers shall wane within the day,
Fear thou not, my mighty sword,
It is the wrath and anger of the Lord.

Before old Dysart's ancient cave,
St. Serf his valiant challenge gave,
Come thou forth if you have breath,
To face a fight unto the death,
And from within did Satan wend,
To give the Saint a horrid end.

Then from the cave, an awful sight,
Emerged into the morning light,
Full nine feet tall, and black as coal,
Of this weak Saint, he'd soon take toll,
No person dared his power defy,
He'd crush him like a common fly!

He laughed, what's this, a common mortal,
Has challenged Satan at his portal?
Get you gone, my leave is given,
Before your very soul is riven.
I fear you not, the Saint replied,
Your evil powers I'll cast aside.

So summon forth your hellish legions,
From deep within your nether regions,
Then darkness fell, and awful sound,
Did issue from beneath the ground,
Deep brimstone pit had Satan caused,
Reaching deep, wherein he housed,

His horrid, evil, monstrous minions,
Which rushed forth from his dark dominions,
Massive things, which shrieked and roared,
Each keen to do his master's word,
The countless thousands which they numbered,
Down on the faithful gathering lumbered.

Though some before the onrush swayed,
The Saint called out, be not afraid!
And from the firmament on high,
An angelic host began to cry,
Behold thou now, this aid we offer,
To the faithful prayer, which thou did proffer.

A wall of fire which then appeared,
Between the warring factions reared,
And being of Heaven's divine construction,
Did cause the awful horde's destruction,
Into the Holy fire they surged,
But not one demon ere emerged!

From all that Satan had employed,
His host was totally destroyed,
Yet, Satan still, the poor folk feared,
As from his damp, dark, lair he reared,
I'll avenge my host a thousand fold,
With powers, awesome to behold.

Miscellaneous

Thou, Saint, who has my power derided,
Upon thy fate be now decided,
You, Dysart folk, doth shed your tears,
I'll rule you for a thousand years,
With great black claws he made to clasp,
Saint Serf within his mighty grasp.

The Lord God's voice, with roar like thunder,
Did rent the very sky asunder,
Bright dazzling bolt of lightning flew,
At charging Satan, straight and true,
Delivering him his last death wound,
To stretch him lifeless on the ground.

The Saint did turn and softly spoke,
To the shocked, astounded, watching folk,
You've seen the power of prayer this day,
Answered in Heaven's noblest way,
Rejoice and praise our heavenly Lord,
Believe you in his blessed word.

Assist me now, this corpse to carry,
To its last tomb, where it may tarry,
For many long and countless years,
This world's now free from all his fears,
Then to deep, dark cave on Dysart's shore,
The Devil's shattered hulk they bore.

They laid him down there deep within,
The cave which they had entered in,
Saint Serf said, people, in thy reach,
Lie huge great rocks upon the beach,
Carry them here and we will sever,
The devil from this world forever.

Their task was done, the entrance sealed,
And one last time the Saint appealed,
I say farewell and journey eastward,
And thou, good folk, make thy way
homeward,
So as the night was gently falling,
He swiftly sped, to do God's calling,
Into the warm summer night,
He vanished swiftly from their sight.

'Sigil De'. Anno 1888.

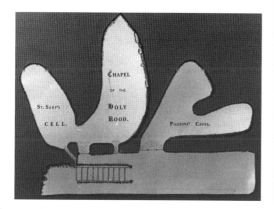

The three caves which now lie in the grounds of the Carmelite Monastery.

One of the Sisters in St. Serf's cave.

Miscellaneous

Born in Dysart

Captain John Pitcairn, Marines, 1760.

John Pitcairn was baptised at St. Serf's Church, Dysart, on 28th of December 1722. He was the youngest surviving child of the Rev. David Pitcairn M.A. (St. Andrews) and his wife Katherine Hamilton, both of well-connected gentry families. He was commissioned Lieutenant in Cornwall's 7th Marines in 1746. When the Marines were established permanently in 1755, he was confirmed in that rank. The following year, he was promoted Captain. He served aboard H.M.S. Lancaster in 1757. In 1771, aged 48, he became a Major in the Chatham division of Marines.

In his early 20s, John had married Elizabeth Dalrymple (1724 - 1809). They had five sons and four daughters. Their Dysart-born eldest son, David, followed his uncle Dr. William Pitcairn to become an eminent physician at Bart's. Robert, born in Burntisland, became a midshipman. In 1767 he was the first to sight the Pacific island named in his honour, but was lost at sea in 1770, aged only 17. William and Thomas joined their father in the Marines, and Alexander became a barrister in England.

In late November 1774, as unrest spread in the American colonies, Major Pitcairn arrived in Boston with some 600 Marines drawn from the Chatham, Portsmouth and Plymouth divisions. He had to contend with a dispute between Admiral Graves and General Gage over landing them, and the fact that they had no proper winter clothing and equipment. The Plymouth Marines had also been sent out with inadequate officers, who could not keep order.

Men were selling their kit to buy the lethal local rum, which killed a number of them. John spent some weeks living in barracks with them to keep them sober. Both respected and popular, he drilled them into an effective force. His concern for his men's welfare was reflected in one of his last acts before going to fight at Bunker Hill: writing a letter to obtain help for some destitute soldiers.

John was billeted on Frances Shaw, a fiercely anti-British tailor, and neighbour of Paul Revere. Remarkably, he won the respect and affection of Shaw and other

Miscellaneous

Bostonians, despite their political differences. He was highly regarded for his integrity, honesty, and sense of honour, and for dealing justly in disputes between the locals and the military.

On 19th April 1775, John Pitcairn was second in command of the troops sent to destroy rebel stores in Concord. At Lexington Green, they came face to face with a body of armed American militia. John ordered his men not to fire, and commanded the rebels to lay down their arms and disperse. But a rebel's musket accidentally discharged, and despite John's efforts, shooting broke out on both sides. The American Revolutionary War had begun.

Their mission in Concord accomplished, the British came under heavy fire on the road back to Boston. John's horse was shot, and threw him. He was forced to march the rest of the way, as the wounded animal had bolted into the American lines, taking with it his brace of richly-decorated Scottish metal scroll-butt pistols. The pistols were presented as a trophy to the American commander Israel Putnam, who used them throughout the war! They are now in Lexington museum.

Putnam was carrying John's pistols on 17th June, at Bunker Hill. The British launched three assaults on the American positions (actually on Breed's Hill) at Charlestown, near Boston, and won the day - but at a hideous cost: 50% killed and wounded. Among the casualties was John Pitcairn. In the summer heat he led Marines - including his youngest son, Thomas (19), a Lieutenant - on foot up the hill for the final assault. While advancing, they crossed another line of infantry, who were being pushed back by heavy rebel fire. John told them, "Break, and let the Marines through!" He waved his sword, and urged his men on: "Now, for the glory of the Marines!"

Then a musket-ball struck him in the breast, and he fell into Thomas's arms. The lad carried his wounded father on his back out of the line of fire before returning to the battle. "I have lost my father!" he said. "We have all lost a father!" some of the Marines responded.

A boat took John back to Boston. He was put to bed in a house on Prince Street. He was fully conscious, but guessed his chances were poor. With stoic courage - and without anaesthetics - he faced the 18th century's most feared enemy: the 18th century doctor. The army surgeons were overworked because of the heavy casualties, so General Gage, anxious to save an officer he greatly valued, had sent a town physician to tend him. Firmly but courteously, John told the doctor not to touch him until he had put his affairs in order. Only then did he agree to have his wound examined. But when the doctor pulled John's waistcoat away from his chest, he suffered a massive haemorrhage. Although the bullet was removed, and his wound dressed, he died several hours later. He was 52.

There is a plaque on Shore Road near St. Serf's Tower commemorating his birthplace.

With acknowledgement to Dr. Marianne McLeod Gilchrist.

Miscellaneous

The engraving above, from the book 'The Kingdom of Fife', printed in 1880, shows a schooner being built at the harbour. Just above the ship, under St. Serf's Tower, stood the old manse of Dysart Kirk. The minister of St. Serf's Church from 1708 to 1757 was the Rev. David Pitcairn, father of Major John Pitcairn, who died at the age of 84 having been a minister for 62 years. A recently discovered letter written by the Rev. Pitcairn to Kirkcaldy Presbytery gives an insight into the living conditions of such an important man and his family almost 300 years ago.

Dysart 29th September 1729.
"Sir, at my accession in the year 1708 I found a very dismal home, yet, having a family, I declined for some time to alarm the parts on that account; thus after some two or three years the late Lord Sinclair being taken ill of the palsy and several misfortunes happening to that family, I reckoned that the world would have thought me ungenerous to have pushed that affair while matters stood in that situation, and so I contented myself rather to give a little patch now and again at my own proper charges till that family should be extracted from their difficulties.

Miscellaneous

I indeed frankly own that some years agone when I necessitated to quit my closet for the convenience of my children and servants and retire to a cold, open garret for the space of two years, the late Lord Sinclair, having heard of it did repair the garret into the form of a closet. Upon this foot the matter stood till the present Lord Sinclair returned from his travels about three years agone, whom I addressed in all civilitie; yea the Presbytrie did interpose that it might be made a lodgeable house, but all to no purpose, upon all of which I have been obliged to take this legal way of a visitation. As to the third ground of my counter-protest, I hope the Reverend committee will consider that ane old house built of mud walls and repaired fourtie years agone must be very much decayed by this time and rendered unlodgeable; upon which I give leave to give only a hint of the present situation; To the doors, about twentie four in number, all rotted and consumed excepting one; secondly, the windows, about twentie in number, scarce any sufficient or proof against wind or weather, to which the manse is much exposed; thirdlie, the mud walls do rot and consume hangings, bedclothes, and everything else, then this house is still moist, cold, unwholesome and breeds much vermin; fourthlie, in that course of fourtie years above said, several floors are rotted and consumed, and the kitchen ruinous wholly, yea, I must add that there's but three bedrooms in the whole of this house, all narrow and confined, so that I have been necessitated these eighteen years and above to lodge my children and two or three several maids still in one little room together, while my wife had a second, and the third I behoved in decencie to keep for any friend, all of which particulars above mentioned I submit to the Reverend committee."

Rev. David Pitcairn.

It is not known if the Rev. Pitcairn's plaintive plea for an upgrade of his manse was ever answered. What is known is that the manse, which was built in 1583, was vacated in 1802 when the new Parish Church was built at Townhead. The new manse was a three storey building in East Quality Street which is still there. The manse at the shore was demolished around 1882.

The stone lintel of the old manse which bears the motto 'MY HOIP IS IN THIE LORD'.
Right, another entrance into the manse also at the side of what is now Bay House.

Miscellaneous

Born in Dysart

John McDouall Stuart
c.1860.

Stuart's birthplace in 1956 before restoration.

John McDouall Stuart was born in Dysart on 7th September 1815. The house where he was born is in what is now known as Rectory Lane. His father was William Stuart, an ex-army officer who came to Dysart in March 1812 to take up the post of Customs Officer at a time when Dysart was a Royal Burgh and the harbour was a bustling port. His salary as Second Officer of the Dysart Salt Collection was £85 a year. John's mother was Mary McDouall of Logan, Wigtownshire.

The young John would have attended one of the several schools in Dysart at that time. The town ran a school and there were various private places of learning. In later years John went to the Scottish Naval and Military Academy in Edinburgh where he qualified as a Civil Engineer. His parents both died within a short time of each other while he attended the Academy. John went to stay with his brother Samuel in Glasgow and it is thought that he continued his studies there.

Because of the poor economic conditions facing Britain at the time, John decided to make a new life for himself and emigrated to Australia in 1838. A book entitled *The Land of Promise* was published in 1838 extolling the climate and attractions of Australia as a place where 'industrious and steady men' could make a prosperous life for themselves. There had also, in 1837, been an appeal sent back to Britain by special ship, of the need in South Australia for land surveyors. John set sail from Dundee on the barque 'Indus' on 13th of September, arriving in South Australia in January 1839. He was then aged twenty-three.

When he landed in Australia, Adelaide was still a rough settlement just over two years old. It appears that John found employment as a draughtsman in a government survey camp twenty miles from Adelaide. Conditions in these camps were rough in the extreme and those living there were quick to learn the bush-man's skills which would stand John in good stead in his later career. John was a short, slightly - built young man but he possessed a strong constitution and adapted himself easily to the rigorous living conditions.

His next recorded engagement was in 1844 when he joined Captain Charles Sturt's

Miscellaneous

exploring expedition as a draughtsman. Sturt was convinced that there was a vast inland sea in the centre of the as yet unexplored continent and was given permission from the Colonial Office to mount an expedition to explore and ascertain the nature of the country in this region. The expedition left Adelaide on 10th August 1844 and did not return for fourteen months, having endured the most terrible conditions of searing heat and a constant lack of water. Some of the aims of the expedition had been met but Captain Sturt, from his observations, no longer believed there to be an inland sea. John McDouall Stuart had been employed as an assistant surveyor but with the death during the expedition of the chief surveyor, he was promoted to this post. Because of Stuart's map and chart making ability during the expedition, Captain Sturt wrote of him in his account of their travels: *"I should be sorry to close without recording the valuable and cheerful assistance I received from Mr. Stuart, whose zeal and spirit were equally conspicuous, and whose labour on the charts did him much credit."*

Not much is known for certain about Stuart over the following two years, but it seems he entered into a partnership with a Mr. Lambeth and took over a firm of Architects and Surveyors in Adelaide. This business appears to have lasted for just over a year and nothing is known of his movements for another two years when reference is made to him in Port Lincoln, 450 miles from Adelaide. There is in existence a survey plan dated 1848 of a station named 'Warrow' near Coffin Bay and signed by Stuart. He was employed as a land surveyor in this area till he moved to the Flinders Range in 1853. It was at this time that he met James Chambers, an Englishman and an early settler who had made his mark as a business man and pastoralist. Chambers hired Stuart to survey land in the interior to find grazing land for cattle and sheep and also, mineral deposits such as copper and gold which could be commercially exploited.

The years 1856 and 1857 saw a great revival of activity in the exploration of the Australian continent. Stuart embarked, in 1858, on the first of six expeditions into unknown country. The first three expeditions were made to survey land, followed by three successive attempts to cross the continent from south to north. On the first journey he was accompanied by two men, including an aborigine, who deserted, and six horses. This was a 1,500 mile round trip into completely new territory.

Journey two was to survey land claims in the region of Chambers Creek. New discoveries were made and they went 90 miles further north than before. The party included Stuart and three men with an unknown number of horses. The third expedition was again to survey land claims and some rather unsuccessful gold prospecting was undertaken. This time the party included Stuart and five men with twelve horses.

The fourth trip led to the great achievement of Stuart's party reaching the centre of the continent. He named the mount there after Captain Sturt but the Governor of South Australia later changed this to Central Mount Stuart, in recognition of Stuart's achievement. This expedition comprised Stuart, two men and three horses. He was awarded the Gold Medal of the Royal Geographical Society for his discovery of the centre of Australia. The fifth expedition in 1860 - 1861 was not so successful as previous ones.

The party was this time forced to return to Adelaide after provisions began to run out. They made eleven unsuccessful attempts to cross impenetrable scrubland at the north of Australia. This was the largest expedition undertaken by Stuart up to this time, with ten men and forty nine horses.

The sixth expedition, started in October 1861, was the most successful and Stuart led his party from Adelaide across the centre of the continent and on to the north coast at the Gulf of Van Diemen, arriving there in July 1862. After a most strenuous journey of over 2,000 miles through stony deserts, swamps, dense bush and grasslands, Stuart's party had to face the return journey, a most exhausting trial for Stuart whose health was giving out. Suffering from scurvy and almost blind, he had to be carried for a considerable time on a stretcher slung between two horses. However, he was to able to make his entry into Adelaide on horseback to be acclaimed the first successful leader of an expedition to cross the continent from south to north. An award of £2,000 was made to him by the South Australian Government, as well as a land grant. Unfortunately, his health was broken by the conditions endured during his explorations. He returned to Britain in 1865, sailing, coincidentally, in another ship called the 'Indus', a larger sailing ship than the one which brought him to Australia 26 years before. On arrival in England, he stayed for some time with the widow of his eldest brother in London. He then moved to Glasgow for a short time to live with his eldest sister, Margaret, wife of John Arthur, a Glasgow business man.

His health worsening, he returned to London and died on 4th June 1866. He was buried in Kensal Green Cemetery. His widowed sister, Mary Turnbull, erected the tombstone which still marks his grave, and which bears the inscription:

TO THE MEMORY

OF

JOHN McDOUALL STUART

SOUTH AUSTRALIAN EXPLORER

THE FIRST WHO CROSSED THE CONTINENT FROM

THE SOUTH TO THE INDIAN OCEAN

BORN 1815; DIED 1866

ERECTED BY HIS SISTER

Miscellaneous

Born in Dysart

Supplement to The Post Sunday Special, Oct. 3d. 1915.

Sergt. JOHN PATTERSON, D.C.M., Dysart.

Sergeant John Patterson was employed as a shafts-man at the Francis Colliery at the outbreak of the Great War in 1914. He was mobilised as a member of the Territorial Army, serving in the 1/7 Black Watch.

He went out to the front in April 1915 as a corporal and was later promoted to sergeant. Because of his mining background he was transferred to the Royal Engineers and was involved in tunnelling under the German defensive lines in order to plant explosives.

After being affected by gassing during his rescue attempt he was attached to the Royal Field Artillery which he was serving in when he was killed in action. The following items are from the Fife Free Press of the time.

Fife Free Press September 4th 1915.

Dysart Territorial Sergeant Gassed.
Mrs. Patterson, 23 Fraser Place Dysart has received information that her husband, Sergeant John Patterson of the 1/7 Black Watch, is in a field hospital in France suffering from gas poisoning. The information was conveyed to Mrs. Patterson in a letter sent by corporal Hugh Patterson, also of the 1/7 Black Watch who states that his brother had gone out to bring in two comrades who had been overcome and succeeded in doing so; but in the process he got a dose of gas which necessitated his being taken to hospital, along with the two men he rescued. Sgt. Patterson was employed as a shafts-man at the Frances Pit then mobilised as a member of the Territorial Forces on the outbreak of war. He went out to France in April as a corporal and has since been promoted to the rank of sergeant. His brother, corporal Hugh Patterson was employed as a miner at the same pit.

Fife Free Press September 25th 1915.

"Fifes Own" First DCM.
Distinction for Dysart soldier.
The distinguished honour of being the first soldier in the 1/7 Black Watch (Fifes Own) to be decorated with the Distinguished Conduct Medal falls to the lot of Sergeant John Patterson, 23 Fraser Place Dysart whose deed of self sacrifice in saving two comrades fully merits the honour which has been bestowed on him.

Miscellaneous

𝔉ife 𝔉ree 𝔓ress October 2nd 1915.

A Modest Hero
Dysart's DCM hero Sergeant John
Patterson of the 1/7 Black Watch, left for
the firing line again on Sunday evening after
spending a few days leave with his wife
and family at 23 Fraser Place. Of a quiet,
retiring disposition, the gallant Sergeant
is a man who hates any fuss and only a few
knew that he had been home from the front.
In order to avoid any display he left the train
at Kirkcaldy and came home by tram, while
the fact that he was in the uniform of a Royal
Engineer, to which he has been attached for
some weeks, instead of the kilt of the Black
Watch, helped to put the few who were on the
look-out for him off the scent. To those who
conversed with him during his brief stay, Sgt.
Patterson had very little to say regarding his
gallant exploit although it was evident he
had not fully recovered from the effects of gas
poisoning.

𝔉ife 𝔉ree 𝔓ress October 16th 1915.

Sergeant Patterson's Bravery
His Majesty the King has been graciously
pleased to approve the award of the
Distinguished Conduct Medal to 1176 Sgt.
John Patterson 1/7 (Fife) Battalion Royal
Highlanders T.F (Attached 179 Co. R.E) :
"For conspicuous gallantry and devotion to
duty at Laboisselle on 26th August 1915. A
non - commissioned officer and a private
descended a mine, but the non-commissioned
officer, overcome by gas, fell to the bottom of
the shaft. The private went to his rescue but
himself collapsed Sgt. Patterson at once
descended to attempt their rescue but he also
collapsed, and though he succeeded in
regaining the surface, had to be taken to
hospital badly gassed." The gallant Sgt. is a
native of Dysart.

𝔉ife 𝔉ree 𝔓ress April 1st 1916.

Dysart's DCM Hero
Honoured by the Townsfolk.
An interesting function took place in the
Normand Memorial Hall, on Saturday
evening, when John Patterson, late
Sergeant in the 117 Black Watch, and now
bombardier in the Royal Field Artillery,
was presented with the DCM and the Royal
Humane Society's Testimonial on vellum
along with a purse of sovereigns subscribed
by the citizens of Dysart. Provost Anderson
presided over a large attendance and was
accompanied on the platform by Bombardier
and Mrs. Patterson. Baillies Irvine and
Macleod, Treasurer Laing, Councillors
Kerr and Barclay. Rev. D.A. Morrison, and
James Herd, Town Clerk.
The Provost congratulated Bombardier
Patterson on his gallantry and assured him
that his fellow townsfolk were all proud of
him. After referring to the pain, suffering
and sorrow and gloom that filled the
hearths and homes of our land, he said it
was dark indeed, but the day would dawn.
The gallant deed of Sgt. Patterson, in
risking his life to save his comrades.
reminded them of the good and beautiful,
and he hoped he would be long spared to
wear the honour with which he had been
bestowed. The Provost then asked Mrs.
Patterson to pin the D.C.M. on her
husband's breast. which she did to loud
cheers. Bombardier Patterson replied
briefly. thanking the Provost and other
speakers for their kind words and the
townsfolk for their generousity.

𝔉ife 𝔉ree 𝔓ress June 1st 1918.

Death Notices
Killed in action on 25th April 1918, Sgt.
John Patterson. D.C.M RF.A .. Beloved
husband of Christina Stuart, 23 Fraser
Place. Dysart.

Miscellaneous

Robert Burns' Connection with Dysart

ROBERT BURNS
1759-1796

Peter Hill was born in Dysart in 1754, the son of James and Mary Hill. Burns became acquainted with Hill when the latter was a clerk in the Edinburgh book-shop of William Creech, the bard's Edinburgh publisher. Later, Hill had his own bookselling business in Edinburgh, becoming also City Treasurer of Edinburgh and the Treasurer of Heriot's Hospital. Burns bought books from Hill and the latter acted on occasion for Burns as a man of business.

The collecting and preserving of old Scottish songs. ballads and lyrics, their polishing and setting to old Scottish tunes, was a passion with Robert Burns until he died. The well known song, 'Up wi' the carls o' Dysart' was just such a re-shaping by Burns of an old Fife folk song.

Up wi' the carls o 'Dysart by Robert Burns

Miscellaneous

The World of John Landless

First published in the Fife Free Press in 1969, these three articles were written by the late Albert Kidd, first secretary of the Dysart Trust. Albert had a vast knowledge of Dysart's history and was moved to write them after the Trust acquired a sketch book of pen and ink drawings made by John Landless in the 1880s. Landless, born in Airdrie, came here on holiday over several years and drew, very accurately, many of the picturesque corners of Dysart which had not changed for centuries.

The Shore, Dysart

In this aspect of our 'ivy mantled tower' and its neighbours, John Landless gives an impression of what a traveller by one of the numerous ferries would see when approaching Dysart; before the coming of the railways in the late 1840s travel by land was difficult and expensive; travel by sea was customary, and in good weather the Forth was a busy highway traversed by many ferryboats crossing and re-crossing between Fife and the Lothians.

   Throughout the centuries the sea has been a main pre-occupation of the people who lived on the margin of the Forth; to many it was a means of livelihood, a source of raw material for the home market and for export - fish and salt; but always present would be the threat of storm and wreck, possible dearth of fish, and the fear of invasion by an enemy, such as the ruthless Vikings, or the Danes, and later the aggressive 'auld enemy' - England.

   To counter this threat of invasion the third, or perhaps the fourth, Lord Sinclair built the defence tower or Steeple on the present site, early in the 16th century, to be used as a protection for his manor house, the Hermitage, some two hundred yards to the north, and also to guard the landing beach edging the Anchorage, that stretch of water lying between the Jetty and the Harbour. The four gun-loops, low down on the south face of the tower, would have been rendered useless if a building had been erected in the gap between Bay House and the house with the 'fore stair' on the right of the picture.

Miscellaneous

The World of John Landless

The gap has remained empty of houses throughout a possible three and a half centuries until our own day; this year (1969) should see the completion and occupation of houses on this site, designed to conform and blend with the older group.

Seafarers were an important part of Dysart's population in the past; the names of ship-masters, mariners, and seamen abound in burgh records, as well as the names of pier and harbourmasters. In the pre-Reformation Kirk of Dysart there was an altar to the Trinty, whose special care was that of the men of the sea; in 1574, after the Reformation, there is note of conveyance of a legacy to the 'alteris trinitas aliquando situati in templo de Desert'.

A drawing of 1778 shows that the largest gallery or loft in the Kirk, belonged to the shipmasters and seamen, and in 1802 a list of the number of seats 'purchased in the intended new Church of Dysart by Publick Bodies' was headed by the Sailors' Society, purchasing 59 seats, including 20 at the dearest price of £2 10/- per bottom room. Next came the Maltmen with 23 seats, and the Weavers with 17.

The salmon nets on the left of the picture remind us of an industry no longer followed in this district, but the story of how Dysart fishermen of 80 years ago showed great skill and courage in a thrilling and successful rescue has been recorded for us:

"Friday November 16th 1888 saw the fiercest storm within living memory; six wrecks were reported between Burntisland and Methil, with an additional two at Inchkeith." Our eye-witness, one of the crowd of Dysart people assembled in great agitation and excitement, perhaps on this very spot depicted by John Landless, continues:

"At six o' clock on Friday evening the gale came on again from the west and a Norwegian brig and a Danish schooner that were driven ashore at Dysart in the afternoon were in imminent danger of destruction. The Norwegian brig struck on the rock known as Partan Craig, about 300 yards east of the harbour, severely damaging her bottom. The Dysart pilot boat, belonging to and manned by John Grubb and John Smith, pilots, assisted by Benjamin Allan, James Allan and Alexander Allan, fishermen, gallantly went to the rescue, and with great difficulty and daring managed to rescue the crew of eight. The townspeople watched tensely the gallant efforts, and many of the people and the coastguards waded to the waist in the raging sea to launch the pilot boat and then drag it ashore with the rescued crew. The brig drifted on to the sands at Dovecot, where she lay fast till Sunday morning, when she was taken off and towed to Leith. The shipwrecked crew were hospitably entertained by Mr. David Owler, newsagent, Dysart.

Meanwhile, the Danish schooner, which had been driven further inshore at the back of the pier, also sustained considerable damage, but on Saturday afternoon was successfully removed from the dangerous position and taken into the harbour by Messrs Foster & Co., shipbuilders, Dysart, who received £80 for saving her, and also repaired the damage done as part of the agreement." A.K.

Miscellaneous

The World of John Landless

St. Serf's Tower 1886

The eighty-foot Tower which dominates the group of houses at present (1969) being restored at the Shore, Dysart, is now called St. Serf's, but older inhabitants, who remember the days before this century began, still call it the Steeple, a name by which it has been known since 1553, when a meeting of the 'neighbours' convened by Bailies John Jackson and David Blair, was held in the 'Stepell', the business under discussion being the amount the custom master should be allowed to charge 'for ilk boll of malt outgiven, or given, said or laid furth the toun.'

The Steeple was also a lookout and defence tower commanding a good view of the widest part of the Forth estuary, and more importantly, the entrance to the firth from the North Sea. Four gun-loops, thought to be copied from those of Ravenscraig Castle a mile westward along the rocky coast, overlooked the only safe landing beach on this part of the shore; on either side nature provided an almost continuous barrier of jagged reefs, not so formidable now as in the days before Frances Colliery spilled its thousands of tons of redd westwards along the coast and blanketed the rocky shoreline.

The word steeple implies that there was a church somewhere beneath it. Masons' marks within the Tower, and also cut on the arches forming the nave of the old kirk have been cut by the same craftsmen, dating tower and kirk at roughly the same period, estimated by experts as being 'early sixteenth century'. There was a church in Dysart before that, however, proof may be found in the Pontifical carried by Bishop David de Bernham on his journeyings through Fife and the Lothians, dedicating or re-dedicating churches in no fewer than 140 parishes within the span of seven years. This Pontifical is now lodged in the Bibliotheque Nationale, Paris, and on its flyleaf, among many similar entries is a record of de Bernham's re-dedication of a church in Dysart on March 26th, 1245, associating it with the name of St. Servanus or Serf, the

Miscellaneous

The World of John Landless

Pictish missionary who had chosen as one of his mission stations the Cave of Dysart, the 'deserta' which gave Dysart its name.

A steeple without a clock would be a matter of serious reproach to the lieges of the sixteenth century; the bailies and council did contrive, however, to acquire a clock in the year 1592, when Henry Kilgour sold his "knock and pertinents, as he has the same presently, to the Town and Kirk of Dysart for the sum of twentie merks." It was evidently not a cash sale, the bailies and council binding themselves or their successors, "to pay the said Henry betwixt this and Michaelmas next comes, and the said Henry to keep her for the year to come."

Before the day of reckoning came along, there presented themselves two young 'brabinaris' (weavers), who wished to become freemen of the Burgh. An agreement was drawn up whereby each promised to pay the sum of ten merks to Henry Kilgour and in return they would be received freemen upon their oath 'sworen according to the use'. In this manner the 'burgus regalis' of five years standing acquired its first clock. One would have looked in vain for a dial indicating the time of day on Henry Kilgour's clock, however. There was no provision for visual evidence of the passing of time. The sound of a bell striking the hours was the utmost that his assembly of gears and levers could achieve; which may give us an explanation of the old Scots word for a clock; the 'knock' was the blow of the hammer as it struck the bell, and the name may have continued in everyday use long after such refinements as a dial and hands were introduced. A.K.

Miscellaneous

The World of John Landless

John Landless evidently had his share of good weather on his summer visits to the Fife coast; one gains the impression from this sketch, as from several others drawn by him, of fleecy clouds in a blue 'lift' and below, in this case, a gentle breeze has set the clothes line demurely dancing.

This view, from the east, is an unfamiliar one of a most familiar group - the cluster of houses lying to the south and east of the Steeple of the Kirk of Dysart. Included in the group are The Anchorage, partly hidden by the more prominent Shoremaster's House, and the sea-facing gable of The Tide-waiter's House, in front of which starts the 'hie-gait', a causeyed wynd leading through the group of houses up into the burgh proper. The houses are the stone replacements of a succession of rude dwellings of wood or turf which in the past would have sheltered the fishers, the colliers, and the salters. In the early 15th century the export of fish was an important factor in the nation's economy, and rules regarding the salting and barrelling of herrings were drawn up by the Scots Parliament regulating the size and construction of barrels. The kind of salt that was to be used was also prescribed.

The production of salt was a flourishing industry for many centuries on both sides of the Forth, establishing itself wherever coal and salt water were readily available, heat being necessary to evaporate sea water contained in the iron salt-pans. Dysart's share in salt production is perpetuated in the nickname, the Saut Burgh, earned, perhaps, not so much because of any remarkable output by the local salters, but more likely through a lease granted to the Burgh of Dysart to collect a 'tak or levy on salt, over a district which extended in an eastward direction to the 'Black Stane in Leven Water'.

The name Pan Ha', like that of Prestonpans suggests to the mind's eye a group of steaming saltpans set up on a level piece of ground, or 'haugh', each with its two attendant salters, who, like the colliers, were bondsmen or slaves, just as much the property of the barons Sinclair as the saltpans or coal heuchs themselves.

Miscellaneous

The World of John Landless

It is hard to comprehend that it is still less than two hundred years since this form of bondage was abandoned, and nominally at least, the serfs were given their freedom. A transaction round about the year 1200 records the sale of slaves to a member of the St. Clair family, when Richard Moreville sold to Henry St. Clair, 'Edmund, son of Bonde, and Gillemichael his brother, their sons and daughters, and the whole progeny descended from them, for three merks.'

To spell the word Pan Ha' in this fashion is a clever compromise chosen in preference to the form which some would regard as rustic and uncouth - Pan Haugh. There can be little doubt that this was the original form; several places in Fife, such as East Wemyss and Leven have their Haugh and Haughgate; further afield Glasgow has its Kelvinhaugh on the River Kelvin; to the west there are the Haughs of Urr; to the north the Haughs of Glass and Cromdale. Throughout the country haughs are to be found where the chance of a 'hall' existing is very remote indeed. While on the subject, it may be time to take another look at Templehall, Muttonhall - and even Abbotshall. It may seem like heresy to suggest that this long-established form is an error, but the proximity of a Mylne-toun, as evidenced in Milton Road, denotes the presence of a water mill and the likelihood of a meadow or haugh on the river bank near by.

To come back to the Pan Ha' of today, a remarkable scene of restoration is now presented to the eye. During the past few months great progress has been made by the contractors; the group-relationship of the buildings, originally formed by fortunate chance and circumstance has not, after all, been spoiled by the new additional houses, and the aspect, particularly from the seashore, is full of charm and interest. It is likely to be as much a magnet to artists and photographers in the future as it has been in the past. A.K.

Miscellaneous

High Street c.1924, looking west towards Rectory Lane. The milk cart is just outside
where Glass's shop was. All of the buildings on the left side were demolished in the
1960s. The single storey buildings at the end of the High Street were at this time the
offices of the Earl of Rosslyn's Collieries.

Miscellaneous

East Port looking down Cross Street 1947. The people with the suitcases could be heading for the bus stop at the top of East Port, or Dysart Station, to go on holiday. The group of men further down at Cross Street, on the right, are outside the Black Bull Pub waiting for it to open.

Miscellaneous

The South School, High Street, being demolished, 1960. Built in 1839, and originally known as the Subscription School, the building bore a plaque with the following inscription: 'By the munificent liberality of Peter Smith, Esq., aided by private subscriptions and a Treasury grant, this building, designed to advance juvenile and infant education, was erected in 1839.' It stood at the east end of the High Street, at the turn off from the High Street down to the Walk. This used to be known as the 'Vennel', an old Scots word meaning a passage way.

In 1874, the Subscription School took the name of Dysart South School, and the Burgh School at School Brae became the North Public School. In 1881 the two schools were amalgamated, the Subscription School becoming the building for the infant division of Dysart Public School. The South School closed in 1916 with the opening of Blairhill School. The building was then used for a variety of purposes. Dysart Band used it for practising, and latterly it was used by Meikle's carpet factory for storage.

Miscellaneous

These two views show the High Street in 1969, just before these buildings were demolished. The right hand side was taken up mostly with Co-op shops.

Miscellaneous

Above, Foggo's Close which ran from
the High Street up to Relief Street. The
photo on the right shows where the
High Street entrance was at the side of
the three storey building. Glass's grocer
shop and Bert Smith's butcher shop were
where the van is parked. 1959.

Miscellaneous

Albert Square, on the left, lay behind the High Street at the Cross and ran up to Orchard Lane. The top of the Tolbooth can be seen on the right. The High Street access was a close where the man is standing in the photo below. The square was demolished in the 1960s.

Miscellaneous

Dysart Harbour 1840.

Miscellaneous

Dysart Harbour and Pan Ha' c.1880.

Miscellaneous

Dysart Harbour 1922.

Miscellaneous

Dysart Harbour 1924.

Miscellaneous

Dysart Harbour c.1895.

Miscellaneous

Harbour, Dysart

Dysart Harbour c.1905.

Miscellaneous

Dysart Harbour c.1910.